AN ESSAY

UPON THE

RELATION OF CAUSE AND EFFECT,

&c.

AN

ESSAY

UPON THE

𝕭𝖊𝖑𝖆𝖙𝖎𝖔𝖓 𝖔𝖋 𝕮𝖆𝖚𝖘𝖊 𝖆𝖓𝖉 𝕰𝖋𝖋𝖊𝖈𝖙,

CONTROVERTING

THE DOCTRINE OF MR. HUME,

CONCERNING

THE NATURE OF THAT RELATION;

WITH

OBSERVATIONS

UPON THE

OPINIONS OF DR. BROWN AND MR. LAWRENCE,

CONNECTED

WITH THE SAME SUBJECT.

LONDON:

PRINTED FOR T. HOOKHAM, OLD BOND STREET,

1824.

ADVERTISEMENT

TO THE

READER.

In the work now presented to the public, I have endeavoured to set down the suggestions, which at different times have occurred to me upon the theory of the relation of Cause and Effect, adopted by Mr. Hume, Dr. Brown, and Mr. Lawrence; and to unfold the train of reasoning which has led me to regard their arguments as illogical, and their conclusions as untrue.

I am fully aware of the difficulties attending such an undertaking, arising both from the popularity of those authors, as well as from the nature of the subject.

Every one must be conscious that the particular forms of expression, in which thoughts of an abstruse and subtle nature are introduced to the imagination, and grow familiar there, are so intimately associated with them, as to appear their just and accurate representative.—But these forms of expression, though clear and satisfactory to the person in whose mind they are so associated, may yet fail in conveying the same ideas with sufficient precision to the understandings of others. In the statement of facts, in moral discussions, in declamation or poetry, this inconvenience can scarcely arise, since they rarely present to an intelligent reader any image which has not under some modification previously passed through his mind, and is not connected with his reflections or experience. But in the subtlety of metaphysics it is otherwise; and moreover, language which was originally framed to suit the commonest occasions of life, is ill fitted, even under the application of the most accomplished intellect, to express the nice abstractions of that science.

These difficulties are the only excuse I can offer for many obscurities of expression, which I fear will be found in the following dissertation, which consists of little more than marginal observations, upon what I cannot but regard as fallacies of the above-mentioned writers, without any pretence of composition or laboured arrangement.

PREFACE.

It is attempted, in the following pages, to controvert Mr. Hume's doctrine on the "Nature of the Relation of Cause and Effect," as set forth in several sections of his "Treatise on Human Nature;" and as confirmed in three sections of his "Essays."—The former work is taken notice of only in as far as it forms a foundation for the latter. But, in as much as some propositions are taken for granted in these latter sections, which serve as the support of all the argument, it could neither be so well answered, nor brought so clearly within the reader's comprehension, as by exposing the fallacies of those assumed premises on which it is founded, and which are to be found at large in the earlier work.

In this respect, Mr. Hume cannot fairly avail himself of the higher esteem he has called upon us to grant to his "Essays" above his juvenile "Treatise;" for, as the conclusions are the same in the Essays as in the Treatise, and as the *medium* arguments used in the Essays are the *conclusions drawn in consequence of great detail of previous discussion in the Treatise*, it is both fair and necessary to examine these details.

It may be, as is hinted in the Advertisement to the Essays,—" that *these de-*" *tails* contain some of those *negligent* " *reasonings that he could have wished not* " *to acknowledge in after life.*"

I shall not, however, readily allow of the advantage of such an excuse; for, as long as the premises that support his matured opinions are only to be found regularly deduced in this unacknowledged work, it is incumbent upon one attempting an Answer to expose them; for, there is no little art, in refusing to adopt the " negligent " reasonings of youth," in a state of advanced judgment, yet covertly making use of a material proposition (that might pass as true, even in many an acute mind, in reading these popular and elegant Essays), which is only supported by the sophistical reasonings of the youthful Treatise, and is evidently adopted in consequence of them. It is also possible, that Mr. Hume might not intend to deny his opinions, in every particular that regarded these points, as he continued to hold the consequential doctrine deduced from them; therefore there may be the less infringement upon the wish he expresses, "*not to be consi-* " *dered as publicly avowing any doctrine not* " *contained in his latter Essays.*"

" That Nature may be conceived to al- " ter her course, without a contradiction," is the material proposition (elicited in the

Treatise, and subsequently assumed in the Essays), on account of which the reader's patience is principally intended to be intruded upon; and which is mentioned in this place, in order that he may perceive the importance of its investigation, previously to his consideration of the more avowed objects brought under his notice, in the answers to the three sections of the Essays, entitled, " Sceptical Doubts con-" cerning the operations of the Under-" standing;" — " Sceptical Solutions of " these Doubts;" and " Of the Idea of " necessary Connexion."

The doctrines contained in these last, lead directly to a scepticism of an atheistical tendency, whose dangerous nature can require no comment, nor any apology for its refutation. Nevertheless, did there seem but sound argument for their support, whatever might be the unhappiness of the opinions that could be inferred from them, I would leave them unnoticed and uncontroverted, imagining there might possibly be an error in the argument, beyond the reach of my discovery; and should content myself in withholding an assent to propositions which my understanding might be unable to refute. Nor at this time of day does the intention of entering into this controversy appear to be useless. It is not many years since Mr. Hume's notions were the occasion of much dispute, on the vsry ground on which I have undertaken it; a dispute which nearly lost the mathematical chair in one of our universities to the present possessor of it, on account of his favouring this doctrine. His opinion, however, as far as it related to any countenance it might afford to the principles of atheism, was defended from the insinuation, by a learned treatise, from the then Professor of Moral Philosophy in the same university. This treatise, whilst it controverts Mr. Hume's opinions in some respects, denies that atheistical inferences may be deduced from them: but I shall endeavour to show, that, in this respect, the author wanted observation and acuteness: neither perceiving the corollaries that go along with the doctrine, nor detecting the sly and powerful sophistry of the reasoning by which they are supported.

Also a modern and living author, of great celebrity, Mr. Lawrence, in his late Lectures, has adopted Mr. Hume's and Dr. Brown's notions of the relation of cause and effect, as containing a proof of the materiality of the soul;—a doctrine of sufficient importance to justify a further investigation of the argument on which it is supposed to be well founded.

In every controversial work, much obscurity appears in an author's arguments, on account of the opinions of his adversary not being distinctly understood; owing either to partial quotation, or mistaken statement: I therefore mean to obviate all chance of any misunderstanding on that ground, by giving the adversary's opinions upon the controverted doctrine in his own words; taking care to leave out only extraneous matter, and to alter the arrangement in such a manner as to form at once a clear and concise, a fair and intelligible view of the whole subject.

AN ESSAY, &c.

INTRODUCTORY CHAPTER.

THE plan I mean to adopt, in order to give a clear view of Mr. Hume's doctrine of the relation of Cause and Effect, in the most concise manner possible, is; first to arrange such quotations from the "Treatise of Human Nature," as will show the opinions there held; and afterwards select some others from the "Essays," in which they are corroborated, and enlarged upon; and which will be sufficient to show, that the doctrines contained in the Treatise are there repeated; with the *addition* of an application of them to the affairs of ordinary life; as affording a ground of scepticism concerning the powers of the understanding having any part to perform in the regulation of her expectations.

The quotations from the Treatise will first show, " what is the doctrine enquired into;" Secondly, the argument, by which Mr. Hume attempts to confute the opinion of the necessity of a Cause, for every beginning of existence; and also the argument he employs in aid of his own doctrine, concerning the ideas we have of the *necessary connexion of Cause and Effect;* and of the *belief* there is placed in such necessary connexion.—Thirdly, the definition of the relation of Cause and Effect; this definition being the object aimed at by the whole argument.

The doctrine enquired into is the necessary connexion of Cause and Effect, and is divided into these two general propositions or queries;

First, " For what reason we pronounce
" it necessary, that every thing whose
" existence has a beginning should also
" have a Cause?"

Secondly, " Why we conclude, that
" such particular Causes must necessarily

"have such particular Effects; and what is
"the nature of that inference we draw
"from the one to the other, and of the
"belief we repose in it*?"

Mr. Hume's method of answering these questions is by adopting a new and sceptical view of the subject, and by attempting to confute those philosophers who were of a different opinion from himself concerning it, by asserting, that it is " neither *intui-*
" *tively* nor *demonstratively* certain that
" every thing which begins to exist must
" have a cause; for in order to show that
" neither intuition, nor demonstration,
" proves the maxim that *whatever begins*
" *to exist must have a cause for existence*,
" let us consider that all certainty arises
" from a comparison of ideas, and from
" the discovery of such relations, as are
" unalterable so long as the ideas continue
" the same. These relations are, resem-
" blance, proportions in quantity, degrees

---

* See Treatise on Human Nature, Vol. 1, Part 3. Concluding Sentences of Sect. 2d, page 116. Sect. 3d, 5th, 6th, 7th, part of Sect. 8th, page 150 to end.

" of any quality, and contrariety; none of
" which are implied in this proposition,
" *whatever has a beginning has also a cause*
" *of existence;* that proposition therefore is
" not intuitively certain." "That the pro-
" position is incapable of demonstrative
" proof, we may satisfy ourselves by con-
" sidering that all *distinct* ideas are *separa-*
" *ble from each other;* and as the ideas are
" separable from each other, and as the
" ideas of Cause and Effect are evidently
" distinct, it will be easy for us to *conceive*
" any object to be *non-existent this moment*
" *and to be existent the next,* without con-
" joining to it the distinct idea of a Cause,
" a productive principle." "The separa-
" tion therefore of the idea of a cause,
" from that of a beginning of existence, is
" plainly possible for the imagination, and
" consequently the *actual* separation of
" these objects is so far possible, that it
" implies no contradiction, nor absurdity;
" and is, therefore, incapable of being re-
" futed by any reasoning, from mere ideas;
" without which it is impossible to demon-
" strate the necessity of a cause." "Ac-
" cordingly every demonstration which has

" been produced for the necessity of a
" cause, is *fallacious* and *sophistical*. They
" all presuppose the existence that begins to
" be an *effect;* but this does not prove that
" *every sort of being must have a Cause.*"

" As the opinion, therefore, that every
" existence must have a Cause, is not de-
" rived from knowledge, or scientific reason-
" ing, it must necessarily arise from obser-
" vation and experience; the next question
" therefore is, *how experience* gives rise to
" such a principle? This question I shall
" sink in the following: Why we conclude
" that such particular causes must neces-
" sarily have such particular effects? Be-
" cause the *same answer will serve for both*
" *questions.*"

The next subject, therefore, which is considered is " necessary connexion;" where it is shown in what way *experience* becomes the foundation of our expectations of similar effects rising from similar causes. The reader must remember that this discussion is supposed to contain the answer to the question, concerning the idea we have of the necessity of a Supreme Cause;

else he might be apt to forget that he has the author's authority for considering the *custom and habit of the mind, arising from an association of ideas, as the only ground of our belief* in the necessity of a *cause* for the beginning of any existence; and consequently for any notion of the necessity for a great Author, Contriver, and Arranger of the universe.

Mr. Hume goes on, " The next ques-
" tion therefore is, whether experience
" *produces* the idea by means of the *under-*
" *standing* or *the imagination*, whether we
" are determined by *reason* to make the
" transition, or by a certain association (of
" ideas) and relation of perceptions."

" If reason determined us, it would be
" on this principle—*That instances of*
" *which we have had no experience must*
" *resemble those of which we have had expe-*
" *rience; for that the course of nature conti-*
" *nues uniformly the same.* Now there can
" be no demonstrative arguments to prove
" that those instances of which we have
" had no experience resemble those of
" which we have had experience."

"*We can at least imagine a change in the course of nature;* reason therefore can never show us the connexion of one object with another, though aided by experience; when, therefore, the mind passes from the *idea* or *impression* of one object to the idea or belief of another, it is not by *reason*, but by certain principles, which *associate together the ideas of these objects*, and unite them in the *imagination.*—The inference, therefore, solely depends on the *union of ideas;*— for,

"After we have observed resemblance in a sufficient number of instances, we immediately feel a determination of the mind to pass from one object to its usual attendant, and to consider it in a stronger light on account of that relation. The several instances of resembling connection lead us into the notion of *power and necessity.*"

"Necessary connexion, therefore, is the effect of this observation, and is nothing

"but an internal action of the mind, or a
"determination to carry our thoughts from
"one object to another."

"The efficacy or energy of Cause,
"therefore, is neither placed in the Causes
"themselves, nor in the Deity, nor in the
"concurrence of these two principles, but
"belongs entirely to the soul, which con-
"siders the union of two or more objects
"in all past instances. Thus objects have
"no discoverable connexion together, nor
"is it from any other principle, but *custom*
"*operating on the imagination*, that we can
"draw any inference from the appearance
"of one, to the existence of the other; and
"all BELIEF in this connexion consists *only*
"*in a lively idea associated to a present im-*
"*pression*; for belief is nothing but an idea
"that is different from a fiction in the
"*manner* of its being conceived. *A present*
"*impression*, transports the mind to such
"ideas as are related to it, and communi-
"cates to them a share of its *force* and
"*vivacity*." The definition of the relation
of Cause and Effect, follows this analysis of

it; and may be observed to be conformable to this notion of a *custom of the mind* being its only foundation.

Thus, 3dly, "We shall now give a "precise definition of Cause and Effect.— "There may be two definitions given of "this relation, which are only different "views of the same object, and make us "consider it either as a philosophical or as "a natural relation: either as a compari- "son of two ideas, or an association be- "tween them."

"We may define a cause to be *an* "*object precedent and contiguous to another,* "*and where all the objects resembling the* "*former are placed in like relations of pre-* "*cedency and contiguity to those objects that* "*resemble the latter.* In the latter sense, *a* "*cause is an object precedent and contiguous* "*to another, and so united with it, that the* "*idea of the one determines the mind to form* "*the idea of the other, and the impression of* "*the one to form a more lively idea of the* "*other.*"

I now refer the reader to the three Sections already mentioned, as found in the 2d Vol. of Mr. Hume's "Essays;" namely,

"Sceptical Doubts concerning the ope-
"rations of the Understanding."

"Sceptical Solutions of these Doubts;" and, "Of the Idea of necessary Connexion."

From these I have arranged some Extracts that will enable us to observe that these doctrines are repeated there, with the addition of an application of them to the affairs of ordinary life, as affording a ground of scepticism concerning the powers of the understanding, in the regulation of its expectations.

That "Nature may be conceived to alter her course, without a contradiction," is the material proposition in both Essays; used as an *argument* to prove, that it is "*custom*" only which forces the "imagination" to *fancy* there is a "necessary connexion between Cause and Effect," with a liveliness, and vivacity of conception, equal to a *firm belief founded on reason*. In the Essays, *the whole of these notions* are supposed to derive their support from the argument, that as we have no knowledge, either *à priori*, or *à posteriori*, concerning the " secrets of Nature;" so our observation of the action of a Cause, affords no ground for the conclusions of reason respecting it.

That the idea of causation is only derived from custom, becomes therefore the premises from which the conclusion is deduced, that " beings can begin their existences of themselves;" which proposition, though not formally repeated in the Essays (and which immediately renders void that for the necessity of a great first Cause, and " *productive principle*" of all things), must tacitly in these Essays be considered as well grounded, because, *as every* foundation whatever, for supposing *any cause* necessary for *any effect*, is denied, and only an influence of " custom on the imagination" is allowed as suggesting a "*fancy of it**;" it necessarily follows, that nothing beyond what this influence suggests can be assigned as any reason why there should be any productive principle for all the contrivances and ends that take place in the universe; it must therefore, I think, be understood that this "juvenile reasoning" was adopted, and acknowledged but too surely, in the latter Essays.

The extracts from the "Essays" are intended to be a counter-part to those taken from the "Treatise," which "show the argument Mr. Hume employs in favour of his own doctrine concerning the necessary connexion of Cause and Effect, and of the Belief reposed in it."—As also the definitions of this relation, which the notions give rise to, and which, with a single exception, will be observed to be little varied from the former ones.

---

* Had ideas no more *union in the fancy*, than objects seem to have to the understanding, we could never draw any inference from Causes to Effects, nor repose belief in any matter of fact.—See Treatise on Human Nature, vol. i. part 3d, p. 134.

I begin the subject with those reasonings which are reckoned the support of the main argument, " Nature may be conceived to alter her course, without a contradiction."

First.—Says Mr. Hume*, " I shall " venture to affirm, as a general proposi- " tion, which admits of no exception, that " the knowledge of the relation of Cause " and Effect is not in any instance attained " *à priori*. Experience then is the founda- " tion of all our reasonings concerning that " relation."

" And, as the first imagination of a par- " ticular Effect is *arbitrary*, where we con- " sult not experience; *so must we also es-* " *teem the supposed tie or connexion between* " *the Cause and Effect which binds them to-* " *gether*, and renders it impossible that any " other Effect could result from the opera- " tion of that Cause †."

---

* Hume's Essays, Vol. 2, Part 1, Sect. 4th, p. 27, 33, 37, &c. Part of Sect. 5. Sect. 7.

† Ibid. p. 30.

Secondly,—" After Experience of the operations of Cause and Effect, our conclusions from that experience are not founded on reasoning, or any process of the understanding; for Nature has kept us at a great distance from all her secrets, and has afforded us only the knowledge of a few superficial qualities of objects, while she conceals from us those powers and principles on which the influence of these objects entirely depends."

Thirdly.—" But notwithstanding this ignorance of natural powers and principles, we always presume, when we see like sensible qualities, that they have like secret powers, and expect that Effects similar to those we have experienced, will flow from them." "This is a process of the mind or thought of which I would willingly know the foundation;" " but enumerating all the branches of human knowledge, I shall endeavour to show that none of them can afford an argument, whence reason may draw a conclusion, that the future must necessarily resemble the past; for all reason-

" ings may be divided into two kinds;
" namely, demonstrative reasoning, and
" that concerning matter of fact and ex-
" perience. That there are no demonstra-
" tive arguments in the case seems evident,
" since it implies *no contradiction that the*
" *course of nature may change;* and that
" an object seemingly like those we have
" experienced may be attended with differ-
" ent or contrary effects;"—for,

" May I not clearly and distinctly con-
" ceive that a body falling from the clouds,
" and which in *all other* respects resembles
" snow, may have the taste of salt, or feeling
" of fire. Is there any more intelligible pro-
" position than to affirm, that all the trees
" will flourish in December and January,
" and decay in May and June?" " The
" bread which I formerly ate nourished
" me; but does it follow that other bread
" must also nourish me, &c.?"

" From causes which appear similar we
" expect similar effects—this is the sum of
" all our experimental conclusions—but it
" seems evident that if this conclusion

" were formed by reason, it would be as
" perfect at first, and upon one instance,
" as after ever so long a course of experi-
" ence; but the case is far otherwise."

" Nothing so like as eggs; yet no one,
" on account of this apparent similarity,
" expects the same taste and relish in all
" of them. Now, where is that process of
" reasoning, which from one instance
" draws a conclusion so different from that
" which it infers from a hundred others?
" When a man says, I have found in all
" past instances such sensible qualities
" conjoined with such secret powers, and
" when he says, similar sensible qualities
" will *always* be attended with similar
" secret powers, he is not guilty of a tau-
" tology, nor are these propositions in any
" respect the same. You say the one pro-
" position is an inference from the other;
" but you must confess the inference is not
" intuitive, nor yet is it demonstrative; of
" what nature is it then?"

" This principle is custom and habit:
" for wherever the repetition of any parti-

"cular act produces a propensity to renew
"the act, we always say this propensity is
"the effect of custom. Custom is the
"great guide of human life; and when we
"say, therefore, that one object is con-
"nected with another, we mean only they
"have acquired a *connexion in our thoughts;*
"and *our belief* (in this necessary connex-
"ion,) is *nothing more* than a conception
"more intense and steady than attends the
"fictions of the imagination; and this
"manner of conception arises from a *cus-*
"*tomary conjunction* with something present
"to the memory or the senses."

The definition of the relation of Cause and Effect is much the same as in the "Treatise;" it is this:

"We may define a Cause to be an ob-
"ject *followed* by another; and where all
"the objects similar to the first are follow-
"ed by objects similar to the second; or, in
"other words, where, if the first object
"had not been, the second never had ex-
"isted."

And again, he has a third definition: " The appearance of a cause always con- " veys the mind by a customary transition " to the idea of the effect. Of this also " we have experience; we may therefore " form another definition of a cause, and " call it an object followed by another, " and whose appearance always conveys " the thought to that other."

CHAPTER THE SECOND.

HAVING now made an abstract of Mr. Hume's Treatise and Essays on the subject of the relation of Cause and Effect, I shall proceed to examine each part in as regular an order as I conveniently can; and endeavour to answer the two questions first proposed, in a more popular, and, I hope, not more illogical method than Mr. Hume has followed, by attempting to prove,

FIRST, That *reason*, not *fancy* and " custom," leads us to the knowledge, That every thing which begins to exist must have a Cause.—SECONDLY, That *reason* forces the mind to perceive, that *similar causes* must necessarily produce *similar effects*.—THIRDLY, I shall thence establish a more philosophical definition of the relation of Cause and Effect.—FOURTHLY, show, in what respects Mr. Hume's definition is faulty.—FIFTHLY, proceed to prove that Nature cannot be supposed to alter her

Course without a contradiction in terms; and, finally, show, that *Custom and Habit* alone are not our guides; but chiefly reason, for the regulation of our expectations in ordinary life.

After this, I shall endeavour to point out some material faults in Dr. Brown's reasoning, tending rather to support Mr. Hume's erroneous arguments, than to repel them: arguments which Mr. Lawrence avails himself of, in the Physiological Lectures, at present before the public; which have drawn so much of its Notice; and upon which I shall not consider it irrelevant to make a few remarks.

SECTION THE FIRST.

First, then, let me show, why Mr. Hume's argument, in favour of the possibility of beings commencing their own existence is sophistical; as well as his attempted confutation of those philosophers who have argued to the contrary. Mr. Hume says, the proposition, " that whatever has a beginning, has also a Cause of existence, cannot be demonstrated, because the ideas of Cause and Effect are "distinct" and "separable;" and it will be easy to conceive "any object to be non-existent this minute," and "existent the next;" without "conjoining to it the idea of a Cause, or a productive principle."—"This imagination is plausible, and may perhaps appear well founded until thoroughly sifted. On a first impression, Causes and their Effects may seem separable, because two things are mentioned; one is distinct from the other, and may be *imagined* separated from it.

They may also *seem* to follow one another, and *time* to elapse between the *operation of the Cause*, and the *appearance of the Effect;* so that during the interval of the supposed period, the effect might be *imagined in suspense*, and so indifferent to existence or non-existence; but upon a strict and rigid attention to the real nature of a thing in opposition to its accidental appearances, one cannot, for a moment, suppose that the circumstances here mentioned, namely, of antecedency of Cause and subsequency of Effect; or of that *distinctness of language* which occasions two words to be used for two ideas; should in any degree render it possible for causes and their effects to exist apart in nature. That it is impossible for them to do so, without involving a direct contradiction in terms, is a proposition I hope to prove in the course of this Essay.

But before examining into this notion, concerning the possibility of effects being held in suspense, and then of being liable to begin their own existence, or, in Mr. Hume's words, " of the separation of the " idea of a cause from that of a begin-" ning of existence," it will be necessary to render the expressions in which it is conveyed more intelligible. This can in no way be done so long as the *definition of the word effect* presupposes a cause; for the supposition of the objection lies, in its being possible for *effects* to be held in suspense: but in order that this should be possible, the meaning of the word *effect* must be altered. Then, if the ideas are altered that lie under the term, according as the varied occasion seems to require, there can be no philosophy; and it never can be insisted on, that the *effects*, which are *supposed to be conjoined* with their causes at one period of time; and to require, in order to their exhibition, those causes or others; and to receive the name of *effects*, on account of requiring causes; can again, upon another occasion, not be *effects*, not require *causes*, be held in suspense, and be *imagined* capable *of beginning their existence by themselves*, without conjoining to them the distinct idea of any " productive principle."—It might as well be reckoned sound reasoning, after defining the figure 2 to be a sign signifying that two units are necessary to its composition, to maintain, that because it stands *singly*, it can be *imagined an unit itself*, without a contradiction; so that it *does not* stand in need of 2 units to its composition:—that is, a word may be taken in two contradictory senses, and then it may be reasonable to predicate of each, affections that belong only to the other; and so to form any contradictory scheme in the world. To make, therefore, any thing like a rational meaning in this sentence of Mr. Hume's, nothing more can be intended by it, than that we should imagine, those existences which we always observe conjoined with others in such a manner, that they *appear* to be their effects, properties, or qualities, to owe them *no real existence or dependence;* and therefore capable of being independent objects, and of beginning their own existence. In like manner, it may be said of *causes*, that although the word signifies something calculated to introduce a certain quality, yet that in fact it does not introduce a new quality; thus naming the object in one sense, and imagining its essence in another sense.

This also is as though we should agree to designate each unit by the figure 1; and to assert, that the union of two units introduces a compound notion, which shall be made known by the sign 2; and on account of this relation, the union of the units shall be called the cause of the compound quality two, under a single term; and the sign 2 shall be named its *effect;*

and afterwards assert, that we can *imagine* the *cause*, that is the *union of the two units*, to exist without, and separate from, the effect, the result 2. All this cannot take place whilst we assign the same meaning to our words; and if we use the terms in different senses, there can be no philosophy.—Therefore, to make any meaning whatever of the proposition, " We may " imagine causes to exist separate from " their effects ;" the objects we call *causes* are not to be imagined as *causes*, but may be supposed *not to cause any thing*, but to exist without *determining their own effects*, or *any others;* that is, causes and their effects are so evidently distinct, that they may be imagined to be unconnected objects, that are *not causes and effects*, and to exist separately without a contradiction, though they are named expressly as signs of the ideas we have, that they are necessary to one another.

Thus, the original question, namely, " Whether every thing which begins to " exist requires a cause for its existence?" resolves itself into two others; viz.

First, Whether objects called EFFECTS, necessarily require causes for their existence? or, whether they may begin to exist with, or without them indifferently?—As also,

Secondly, Whether any objects whatever, without being considered as having the *nature of effects*, can begin their existences?

It may be plainly seen, that the first of these questions is sunk in the latter, because, if objects *usually considered as effects* need not be considered as effects, then they are forced to begin their existences *of themselves:* for, conjoined or not to their causes, we know by our senses that they do begin to exist: we will, therefore, immediately hasten to the consideration of the second question, which may be stated in the following terms: Whether every object which begins to exist must owe its existence to a cause?

Let the object which we suppose to begin its existence of itself be imagined, abstracted from the nature of all objects we are acquainted with, saving in its capacity for existence; let us suppose it to be *no effect;* there shall be no prevening circumstances whatever that affect it, nor any existence in the universe: let it be so; let there be nought but a blank; and a mass of whatsoever can be supposed not to require a cause START FORTH into existence, and make the first breach on the wide nonentity around;—now, what is this starting forth, beginning, coming into existence, but an action, which is a quality of an object not yet in being, and so not possible to have its qualities determined, nevertheless exhibiting its qualities?

If, indeed, it should be shown, that there is no proposition whatever taken as a ground on which to build an argument in this question, neither one conclusion nor the other can be supported; and there need be no attempt at reasoning.—But, if my adversary allows that, no existence being supposed previously in the universe, existence, in order to be, must *begin to be*, and that the notion of *beginning an action* (the being that *begins* it not supposed yet in existence), involves a *contradiction in terms;* then this *beginning* to exist cannot appear but as a *capacity some nature hath* to alter the presupposed nonentity, and to act for itself, whilst itself is not in being. —The original assumption may deny, as much as it pleases, all cause of existence; but, whilst in its very idea, the commencement of existence is an effect predicated of some supposed *cause, (because the quality of an object* which must be *in existence to possess it,)* we must conclude that *there is no object which begins to exist, but must owe its existence to some cause.*

For this reason it is, that the answers to Dr. Clarke and Mr. Locke are unsound, in as far as they are an endeavour to show, that their arguments are altogether sophistical.—Mr. Hume objects to them, that the existence supposed to begin by itself, " is not to be considered as an *effect;* and that these authors assume what is not granted, viz. that the existence in question requires *a cause;*" as where Dr. Clarke shows it is an absurdity to imagine an object its *own cause,* and

Mr. Locke asserts that it is equally so, to conceive of *nothing* as a cause. It is undoubtedly true, that these authors assumed that which was in question; namely, that every existence must have a cause: but, as every thing not yet in existence, *to exist at all*, must *begin*, and as the *beginning* of any thing must always be supposed, by the *nature of the action*, to be a quality of something in existence, which existence is yet DENIED by the statement of the question, these philosophers felt the involved absurdity so great, that they passed over the first question as too ridiculous, probably, to consider formally; then showed, that the mind of man was forced to look upon all things which begin to exist as *dependent* QUALITIES; and thus, that an object could neither depend upon *itself for existence*, nor yet upon *nothing*.

Let it be remembered, too, that although Mr. Hume inveighs against this method as sophistical, by conceiving it begs the question, yet his own argument, the whole way, consists in the possibility of imagining an *effect* " *non-existent* this minute," and "existing the next;" and does not himself consider any other "sort of being" possible; and has no other way of supporting his own notion of the beginning of existence by itself, except under the *idea of an effect in suspense;* which is still a *relative term*, and begs the question for the necessity of its correlative, i. e. its *cause,* just as much as he asserts his adversaries do, whom he declares to be illogical reasoners.

If then (as I hope I have shown) all objects whatever, which *begin to exist,* must owe their *existence to some cause,* those we usually consider as *effects* CANNOT be held in suspense; suddenly alter their nature; be "*non-existent* this minute, and existent the next;" and, though always introduced as *qualities of other objects,* be easily separated from the ideas of their causes, and require no " productive principle."

" That Cause and Effect are distinct and separable;" so " that any object may be conceived, as therefore *capable of begin-*

ning its own existence," must be considered as among the notions adopted in *the Essays:* what else is the meaning of such propositions as these: " There appears not " throughout all nature, any one instance " of connection, as conceivable by us;" " one event follows another," "but we never can observe *any tye between them,* &c.*" Indeed, the not admitting " *any relations of ideas,*" or " *any reasonings a priori,*" (so as to be capable of supporting the idea of CAUSATION as a *creating principle* absolutely necessary in the universe) is but repeating " the *juvenile ideas*" of the Treatise, and " *casting them anew in these later pieces*†."

Before I proceed further, I wish my reader to grant the proposition, " That a Being cannot begin its existence of itself;" because I mean to make use of it in my further reply to Mr. Hume's doctrines; and, unless this step is allowed, I can make no further progress in this argument.

* Essays, Sec. 7. p. 77.
† See advertisement to the Essays.

SECTION THE SECOND.

We will now proceed to the second part of the original inquiry; that is, Why " we conclude that such particular Causes must necessarily have such particular Effects; and what is the nature of that inference we draw from one to the other, and of the belief we repose in it? The question, however, ought to stand thus, " why LIKE CAUSES must necessarily have LIKE EFFECTS? because what is really enquired into, is the *general notion of necessary connexion*, between *all like* Cause and Effect; and by thus putting the question respecting *particulars only*, although they might be included in an universal answer, yet no answer applicable to them MERELY, could authorize an *universal axiom*. The manner of stating the enquiry in *the Essays*, is also too vaguely expressed, (although it be evident that it is the *general relation* which is enquired into.) Mr. Hume says, " we will now enquire, how we arrive at the *knowledge of Cause and Effect**." *It ought to be stated*, how we arrive at the knowledge of the *necessary connexion*, between *like* Cause and Effect?

---

* Essays, Sec. 4. p. 27.

Let it be remembered, that Mr. Hume says, "this principle is nothing but custom and habit;" that "belief in necessary "connexion is nothing but an intense "and steady conception, arising from "the customary conjunction of the ob- "ject with something present to the me- "mory or senses; that when flame and "heat, cold and snow, have always been "conjoined together, there is such a cus- "tomary conjunction between them, that "when flame and snow are anew present- "ed to the senses, the mind is carried by "custom to expect heat and cold."

"That *reason* can never show us the "connexion of one object with another, "though aided by experience; for we can "at least *conceive a change in the course* "*of nature*. That necessary connexion is "nothing but an internal act of the mind, "determined to carry its thoughts from "one object to another." Thus *necessary connexion* of cause and effect is only a custom of the mind! *Power* is only a custom of the mind! Expectations, and experience, are only customs of the mind!

The consequence of which doctrine is, that as a *custom of the mind* is entirely a different circumstance from the *operation of nature*, we may " *conceive* " at least the contrary of what we have been accustomed to may take place,—we may conceive the " course of nature to change."

Now it is my intention to shew, in contradiction to these ideas of Mr. Hume, that it is *Reason*, and not *Custom*, which guides our minds in forming the notions of necessary connexion, of belief and of expectation*.

* I conceive it impossible to have a complete conviction that every Effect is inherent, or contained in its Cause, until the mind be imbued with the knowledge, that objects are but unknown circumstances in Nature, when unperceived by the senses; which when perceived, exhibit their appropriate qualities accordingly; and which then appear in certain defined masses, as to the different senses they affect, as to their figure, &c.; and receive an arbitrary name for their assemblage. They must have also among each other certain proportions. When these unknown circumstances, (or affections, or substances,) in nature, *mix*, and are thereby *altered, the qualities which affect the senses* are in the *same proportions* altered, and are necessarily included in those objects as their Effects. But this part of the subject, is of such moment that a separate consideration of it is intended.

In order to this let us bear in mind the reasoning already adduced in the foregoing Chapter, and it thence immediately follows, that objects which we know by our senses do begin their existences, and by our reason know they cannot begin it of themselves, must begin it by the operation of some *other beings* in existence, producing these new qualities in nature, and introducing them to our observation. The very meaning of the word Cause, is *Producer* or *Creator;* of Effect, the *Produced* or *Created*—and the idea is gained by such an observance of nature, as we think is efficient in any given case, to an *experimentum crucis.*

Long observation of the invariableness of antecedency, and subsequency, is not wanted; many trials are not wanted, to generate the notion of *producing power.*

One trial is enough, in such circumstances, as will bring the mind to the following reasoning.

Here is a new quality, which appears to my senses:

But it could not arise of itself; nor could any surrounding objects, but one (or more) affect it; therefore that one, (or more) have occasioned it, for there is nothing else to make a difference; and a *difference* could not "*begin of itself.*"

This is an argument, which all persons, however illiterate, feel the force of. It is the only foundation for the demonstrations of the laboratory of the chymist; which all life resembles, and so closely, in many instances, that the philosopher, and the vulgar, are equally sure of what cause is absolutely necessary to the production of certain effects; for instance, each knows that in certain given circumstances, *the closing of the Eye* will eclipse the prospect of nature; and the slight motion of reopening it, will restore all the objects to view. Therefore, the Eye (in these circumstances,) is the *Cause* or *Producer of vision*. ONE trial would be enough, under certain *known* circumstances*. Why? not from "*custom,*"

---

* When more trials are needed than ONE, it is in order to *detect* the circumstances, not to lay *a foundation for the general principle,* that a LIKE Cause repeated, a LIKE Effect will take place.

because there has been *one trial only;* but from *Reason,* because vision not being able *to produce itself, nor any of the surrounding objects by the supposition;* it is the *Eye* which must necessarily perform the operation; for there is nothing else to make a difference; and a different quality could not " *begin its own existence.*" It is this sort of REASONING UPON EXPERIMENT, which takes place in every man's mind, concerning every affair in life, which generates the notion of Power, and necessary Connexion; and gives birth to that maxim, " *a like Cause must produce a like Effect.*" The circumstances being supposed the same on a second occasion as on a former one, and carefully observed to be so; the Eye when opened would be expected to let in light, and all her objects. " I observe (says the
" mind) in this or any other case, all the
" prevening circumstances the same as be-
" fore; for there is nothing to make a dif-
" ference; and a difference cannot arise
" without something to occasion it; else
" there would be a *beginning of existence*
" by itself, which is impossible."

It is this compound idea, therefore, *the result of the experience of what does take place upon any given trial*, MIXED with the *reasoning that nothing else could ensue*, unless on the one hand, *efficient causes were allowed for the alteration;* or, on the other, that things could "*alter their existences* FOR THEMSELVES;" which generates the notion of *power or "producing principle,"* and for which we have formed the word.

It is in vain to say that a habit of association of ideas from observing "*contiguity in time, and place,*" between objects is all we know of *power;* a habit of the mind will not *begin existence*, will not *introduce a quality*. The really philosophical method of viewing the subject is this: that objects in relation to us, are nothing but masses of certain qualities, affecting certain of our senses; and which, when independent of our senses, are *unknown* powers or qualities in nature. These masses change their qualities by their mixture with any other mass, and then the corresponding qualities determined to the senses must of course also change. These changed qualities, are termed *effects*; or *consequents*; but are really no more than NEW QUALITIES arising from *new objects*, which have been formed by the *junctions of other objects* (previously formed) or might be considered as the *unobserved qualities* of *existing objects*; which *shall be observed when properly exhibited.*

If then an existence now in being, *conjoined with any other*, forms thereby *a new nature*, capable of exhibiting *new qualities*, these new qualities must enter into the definition of the objects; they become a part of their natures; and when by careful experiment, or judicious observation, no new prevening circumstances are supposed to make an alteration in the conjunction of the same bodies, the *new qualities*, that are named *effects*, are expected without a doubt to arise upon every such conjunction; because, they as much belong to this *newly combined nature*, as the original qualities did to each separate nature, before their conjunction. So little is custom the principle of cause and effect, that if upon the *first* and original trial of the element of fire, all surrounding circumstances were put away from having any influence over it, saving the body it destroyed; that power of *discerptibility* would be ever after considered as one of its qualities; as much as its colour or its light, or its warmth, without the presence of which, it would not be fire.

This conjunction with a grosser material than itself, is the new circumstance, on which it exhibits its essential and permanent quality of discerptibility to the senses; now if the trial be complete, when upon a second occasion an object having the same sensible qualities as fire hath, known also to have been elicited from the same prevening circumstances, meets with the same gross body as heretofore, it must of *necessity* consume it. There is nothing to make a *difference*. A *difference* is an *Effect*, a *change of being*, an *altered existence*, an existence which *cannot* " *begin* of itself" any more than any other in Nature; could the fire be supposed not to consume the gross body, there would be a *difference* of qualities, that is, new qualities, which by the data there is no cause for. The original circumstances, of which fire is the compound Effect, from which it results as a *formed object*, are supposed to be ordered the same as on a former occasion; these are necessarily compelled to be attended with the same effects or combined qualities; otherwise there would be the " *beginnings* of *existence*" by themselves, which has before been shown to be impossible. But the *combined qualities*, are the whole qualities that fire in every circumstance, is capable of producing. Meeting, therefore, with a gross body, which on any one occasion, in certain circumstances, it once consumed; under the same circumstances, it must necessarily again consume it. That DIFFERENCES OF EXISTENCE cannot begin of themselves; is therefore the second conclusion supposed to be established.

" *Antecedency* and *subsequency*," are therefore ~~im~~material to the proper definition of Cause and Effect;" on the contrary, although an object, in order to act as a Cause, must be in Being antecedently to such action; yet when it *acts as a Cause*, its *Effects* are *synchronous with that action*, and are *included in it;* which a close inspection into the nature of cause will prove. For effects are no more than the new qualities, of newly formed objects. Each conjunction of bodies, (now separately in existence, and of certain defined qualities,) produces upon their union those new natures, whose qualities must necessarily *be in*, and *with them, in the very moment of their formation.*

Thus *the union of two distinct natures*, is the *cause, producer* or *creator* of another; which must instantly, and immediately, have all its peculiar qualities; but the cause has not acted, is not completed, till the *union* has taken place, and the new nature is formed with all its qualities, *in*, and *about it*. *Cause producing Effect,* therefore, under the strict eye of philosophical scrutiny, is a *new object* exhibiting *new qualities;* or shortly, the formation of a new *mass of qualities*. A *chain of conjunctions of bodies*, of course, *occupies time;* and is the reason why the careless observation of philosophers, enabling them to take notice only of some one distinct effect, (after perhaps innumerable successive conjunctions of bodies,) occasions the mistake, by which they consider *subsequency of effect*, as a part of the *essential definition* of that term; and *priority*, as *essential* to the nature of Cause.

As a short illustration of the doctrine unfolded, let us take the idea of nourishment, considered as the effect, subsequent to the taking of food, its cause. Here the *nature* of nourishment, is *a process* which begins to act immediately that food is in conjunction with the stomach. "That we are nourished;" is only the last result of a continuous chain of causes and effects, in formation from the first moment the food enters the stomach, to that, in which every particle is absorbed and deposited in the proper place in the body. Here, the capacity of food to exhibit certain qualities, when in conjunction with the body, is shown; the nature of the human body, to exhibit certain other qualities, in consequence of that conjunction, is also shown; but the *effect of nourishment*, being *subsequent* to, and at such a distance of time from, the original Cause, is only so, on account of its being the effect of a vast number of causes, or unions of objects in succession, of which the union of the stomach and the food was first in order.

Our deficient observation, is apt to prevent our taking notice of the 2d, 3d, or indefinite number of effects; which arise in consequence of as many conjunctions of objects.

But the first, and other *effects* successively, are as much and entirely synchronous with their *causes*, as any other quality of any single object, which is always exhibited along with it.

2dly. It is also quite immaterial to the definition of this relation, whether an untried, or unobserved quality, be called *quality*, or *effect*. The unknown or at present undetermined quality, which is termed an effect, might always change its place with some *known quality*, and not bear the name of effect; and *vice versa*: Thus, a blind man may call the object which warmed, or burned him, fire; but his eyes being supposed suddenly to open, he would consider the flame and its brilliant colour as the *effects* of fire; whilst he who sees fire constantly, being able always to take notice of its flame and colour, considers them as the constant and unvarying *qualities* of fire, and which render the substance before him worthy of bearing that name; but the quality of burning, which he does not *constantly* experience, he names an *effect* or *consequence* of fire previously being in existence. But the true method of looking upon the subject is this—that fire, in order to deserve the name it bears, must comprehend all its qualities *tried* and *untried; observed* and *unobserved; determined* and *undetermined;* it deserves the name only on account of its being a certain defined object; *elicited from certain causes observed to be efficient to its production;* and by the very conditions of the question, is allowed to be *the same*. But an object is nothing else (in relation to *us*,) than a mass of peculiar qualities; and when observations inform us, that any known mass is produced by similar circumstances, on various occasions; such mass or object must necessarily contain all its qualities, and be equal to exhibit all its effects in hitherto untried events. Upon any occasion where we are either certain, or have a high probability, that an object presented to us is truly similar to a former one, and was created by the same causes; we expect all tried qualities to be the same as before, and any *untried* quality, (that is, any quality not in present operation, though previously ascertained,) must belong ever after to its definition. All that is necessary is to be correct, as to the prevening or influencing circumstances which gave *birth to the object*. They being the same on any two or more occasions, the object elicited must necessarily be the same—but it is not the same, unless it hath all its *qualities*, and no other than its qualities. Therefore fire, in order to have a right to the sign of the word fire, for an expression of its attributes, in order to be a " *like cause,*" must of necessity burn as much as it must be red, otherwise the red object were not fire; and *could not have been produced by those causes that elicit that element.* I mean therefore to conclude, that Effects are but the qualities of an object not experienced by some of the senses of the human frame, whilst certain others at present touch it; *the knowledge of which last*, being joined to the observation of the WHENCE the object was produced, beget the knowledge of what new untried qualities may be expected in future under given circumstances. It becomes therefore part of the definition of fire to burn certain bodies, to melt others; of bread to nourish the human body; of snow to be cold, and white; and these qualities they must have, in order to compose that entire *enumeration of qualities*, for which appropriate names have been formed, and to the exhibition of which similar and efficient causes have been in action.

If it should be said, that in considering objects as masses of combined qualities, the *result* of like Causes previously in action, we beg the question not yet supposed to be granted,—I answer; that *like* Causes, that is, *like* objects, are by the supposition admitted, and then the question arises, whether it is demonstrable they must have like effects or qualities, *under like circumstances in future?* I answer, they must have like effects, or qualities, because there is nothing else *given* that can be supposed to make a difference; and a difference of qualities could not arise of *itself*, could not begin its own existence; and I add, not only, there is nothing else *supposed* that can make a difference; but that when we also know that in the FORMATION of any object no difference took place; then, *there is no ground whatever*, for imagining the *possibility* of an *alteration* in *the effects of that object*. But although it be very difficult in the analysis of this question, not to use the word *cause* in its intended sense, before the definition of the word is given, and although it be true that in this last observation I may have done so in saying, *that objects must be the same which are elicited from like causes,* i.e. *from the junction of like prevening circumstances*; (and which position will be fully borne out in the process of the argument;) yet a fastidious reader may omit every such reference to the notion of Cause; for the argument is perfect without it, and stands thus:

Effects are nothing but those *same conjunctions of qualities*, which in other words are admitted as *similar causes*, in the supposition of the question. The objects (whose *union is necessary* to a given result,) must certainly exist, *antecedent* to such an union. But it is *in their* UNION, there exists those *newly formed objects*, or masses of qualities called *Effects*, which are therefore *identical* with the *similar cause;* for in *this union*, Cause and Effect are *synchronous*, and they are but different words for the same *Essence*. Fire and wood must be antecedent to combustion, no doubt; but in the *union of Fire and Wood*, there exists immediately *combustion* as a new event in nature;—also in this union exists the similar *cause* allowed by the *data*, whilst combustion is also termed the *Effect* of the union of Fire and Wood; but, however termed, an *effect*, is in fact a new but similar object as heretofore. A *similar* mass of qualities, in kind, which cannot therefore be a *different* mass of qualities in kind.—Equals added to equals upon any two occasions, the whole must be equal; add equal qualities to equal qualities, the sum of the qualities must be equal upon every repetition of the junction;—and the *sum* must be the *same result* taken *twice over*, not two *different*, or possibly *altered sums*. Therefore I repeat, that in the consideration of the nature of Cause and Effect, it is immaterial whether the yet unframed qualities of objects, previous to their junction, be named *effects;* they are to be considered as qualities; and qualities may be considered as *effects*, under any circumstances that prevent their usual exhibition. Effects when developed are no more than qualities; and qualities previous to their developement are in our imagination considered as Effects.

3dly. Again, it is immaterial to the definition of the relation of Cause and Effect, that we are not acquainted with the "secret powers" of natural objects, either before or after experience; for when we find, that in any distinct and given circumstances they put on certain qualities to the senses, their secret powers and properties must be qualified in all *like circumstances* to be the same, and are obliged to be so; because no contrary qualities could " begin their existences of themselves;" and by the *supposition* there is no *cause in the circumstances*, to give rise to any *differences in the qualities*. Indeed, Mr. Hume makes a great mistake in supposing it necessary to demonstrate, in every particular instance, what *particular* Effect must necessarily flow from its object, in order to gain the idea of *necessary Connexion*. The *how* and the *why* have nothing to do with the general reasoning affecting the general proposition; for " whether like Causes shall produce like Effects" is *not* a question exactly the same as whether " such particular causes shall have such *particular* effects? which Mr. Hume seems to consider as precisely of the same import*; whereas *one is a general* question, which however answered, in the *affirmative* or *negative*, would apply to *particulars*. But supposing in each *particular* instance under our notice, we could descry the " *secret powers of nature*," the general question concerning *all* like causes would still remain unanswered; and an universal conclusion could not logically be deduced from the particular

---

* Compare Sec. 4. p. 30, with Sec. 4. p. 34.

premises concerning it: as will be more fully argued in the discussion upon Dr. Brown's reasoning.

If it should be asked, (as Mr. Hume presently does,) how is it known when objects are similar upon any two occasions; the "sensible qualities may be the same, and not the *secret powers, upon which the Effects depend?*" I answer, this is to *shift* the question from the examination of *like Causes supposed*, to the consideration of the *method whereby their presence* may be *detected**. But this difficulty is met, and considered in, its proper place; I shall only here say, that as the *secret powers* are the real external unknown Causes in Nature, which determine the sensible qualities, as well as *every other Effect*; so when we find the sensible qualities the same on any two occasions,

---

* I should not here have taken notice of this objection, but that as Mr. Hume does suddenly shift the question, so I would not appear to avoid an answer to it: otherwise it is something too early to enter upon the subject; obliging me to make use of my argument previously to its complete developement. But the reader may pass over to the next Section if he please.

we are sure the secret powers are similar *thus far*, and therefore fitted to exhibit their further similar effects;—(or *combined secret powers and sensible qualities;*) and although some *unobserved* cause might creep in to alter the object, whilst appearing the same, yet this we do not *imagine* when we are not aware of it, especially in cases where the same sensible qualities have been regularly exhibited along with like secret powers; for this regularity is perceived as an *Effect*, for which there must be a proportional *Cause*, and begets a proportional belief accordingly.—We argue from the *regular Effects*, (the sensible qualities;) to the *regular Causes*, (the secret powers;) which having been equal to certain other *Effects or properties*, we expect again the same, under similar circumstances.—We argue from the regular *ends* nature keeps in view, up to nature's God, who ordained them, and who must be supposed still to continue true to those ends; and along with the grander operations of nature, we may often in many cases observe our own actions, and those of others, conspiring *only* to fashion similar objects. But when the *secret powers,* and sensible qualities, are known, *or supposed the same*, the conclusion is demonstrative; *so must be the Effects.* Whilst, were it possible to know the secret powers in each *particular* past instance, *universal* truth would not thence result. Neither has Mr. Hume any right to make this argument; because to conceive " there may be secret " powers which may change the Effects, " dependent on them," is to make use of the relation between Cause and Effect, as of a really necessary connexion, in order to oppose his adversary : a principle which he previously refuses to admit. Also the objection forms an illogical argument in another way. For it virtually draws a general conclusion from *two negative premises.* To assert, that like sensible qualities merely, will NOT produce like Effects; and, that *like sensible qualities* are NOT *like Causes*, is to separate the middle term both from the subject and from the predicate of the general question. By *such an argument* Mr. Hume is certainly right in supposing, that REASON cannot support " *our conclusions concern-* " *ing the operations of Cause and Effect.*"

Having thus cleared a way, towards the comprehension of this relation of Cause and Effect, we will proceed to a definition of those terms in the next Section.

SECTION THE THIRD.

A Cause, therefore, is such action of an object, as shall enable it, in conjunction with another, to form a new nature, capable of exhibiting qualities varying from those of either of the objects unconjoined. This is really to be a producer of new being.—This is a generation, or *creation*, of qualities not conceived of, antecedently to their existence;—and not merely an "*idea always followed by another*," on account of a " customary association between them."

An Effect is the produced quality exhibited to the senses, as the essential property of natures so conjoined. Necessary connexion of cause and effect is the obligation qualities have to inhere in their objects, and to exhibit their varieties according to the different human senses with which they come in contact. Power is but another word for efficient cause, or " productive principle;" and signifies the *property* which lies in the *secret nature of objects*, when unobserved by the senses, and which determines the qualities that can be exhibited to them upon every new conjunction.—An *object* may be defined, a *combined mass of qualities;* the result of proportional unknown circumstances in nature, meeting with the human senses.

But Mr. Hume's three definitions of the relation of Cause and Effect are, in many respects, faulty, and not borne out by his own arguments; for he defines a Cause " an object followed by another, and where " all the objects similar to the first are fol- " lowed by objects similar to the second." —Now, if he means an object that will in *future*, as in *past* times, be always followed by another; an *invariable* necessity in the antecedent to be followed by its subsequent, his whole argument tends to prove the *contrary*, and to show that experience has power to answer for the *past* only, and cannot for the future; for, that we may conceive a " change in the course of nature," and that imagination supplies only the notion of *invariable* expectation from "custom;" that this is the sense of the passage containing the original definition, we may be sure of, from what follows; for he goes on to say, " or in other " words, where if the first object had not " been, the second never had existed;" but this idea expresses a much stricter necessity of connexion than does the relation of any number of objects, which had only followed each other in *past time*, however often their antecedency and subsequency had been repeated. Such a necessity is contradicted the whole way by the argument. It is quite another sentiment, from that which arises from the ideas of always *before and after*. That which requires another object to its existence, must be *necessarily connected* with it; and I contend that it is so connected, as a *new quality* of an altered mode of existence. But Mr. Hume says, it is only connected, as an invariable subsequent, must always be understood to require its invariable antecedent. —But I retort, Why does the definition assume more than the argument can possibly bear out?

How can the *invariableness* of the future be answered for by the experience of any invariableness in the past? It is truly impossible that it should be so. Custom can only, at the most, lead us to *expect* that the future would be similar to the past; but it never could so sufficiently answer for it, as to enable us to form a definition concerning its *absolute* INVARIABLENESS *of phœnomenon.*

Indeed, in many cases there are *single* exceptions to *universal* experience, and to any habit of expectation founded on it; which at once proves Mr. Hume's definition to be erroneous; for hence the *invariableness* of the sequence becomes altered, and custom shown to be utterly incapable of affording an *universal definition*, of the relation in question.—Now, *experiment* is what decides as to a real and necessary cause, under given circumstances.—When an event happens under one set of circumstances, not under another in all respects the same, save ONE; *that one* is a *true cause*, and a *necessary one;* and under the same circumstances, it must be invariably wanted to that end; and every mind feels it so, because it perceives that an *alteration* could not begin of itself. This, and nothing but this, is a *strict necessity*, and can enable the mind to predicate for the future as for the past.

But the first definition is also faulty in another instance; because in every just definition, the ideas that are included in the terms, must not suit any other object. Now many objects are invariably antecedents and subsequents, that are not Causes and Effects; and it can be no good definition, to warrant the arguing in a circle, which *this definition* evidently does.

The second definition is also erroneous, because although similar causes must have similar effects, yet *diverse* causes may produce the same effects also—therefore the *second object might exist* without the first, by the operation of any other cause efficient to it*. The third definition, viz.

* I make this remark however, rather with respect to Mr. Hume's notion of Cause than my own; in order to

" an object followed by another, and whose
" appearance always conveys the *thought*
" *to that other*," does not differ materially
from the first—yet it is worthy of observation, that the thought always being carried by the appearance of one object to the idea of another, proves nothing but *an accidental, though strong association of ideas;* and is in like manner objectionable, on account of *suiting other objects than the thing defined*. Every *Andrew* is not necessarily " *Simon Peter's Brother*," although my thought always recurs to that idea, upon every mention of the name of *Andrew*.

SECTION THE FOURTH.

It follows then from the definitions given in the preceding section, and the reasonings on which they are formed, that were a body, in all other respects resembling snow, to have the taste of salt and feeling of fire, it would be an extraordinary phœnomenon, no doubt; and one which might for

shew there is an inconsistency between his argument and his definition; for *diverse antecedents* might invariably be *followed* by *similar subsequents;* then, in each separate case the second object might exist without the first.

ought we know take place, but it would not be snow; and such a body could not fall from the clouds but by new causes efficient to its formation;—it would, therefore, be entirely a different object, and would require a new name; and the phœnomenon could offer no ground for the conclusion, that *reason* does not afford an argument, for the expectation of similar effects from similar causes.

Nature, it is true, varies all her operations; but not in a manner that can ever make it appear otherwise than a contradiction to reason, that it should be through interferences with her regular course. For instance, something similar to the case imagined does take place; we all know that various substances fall from the clouds; but they are all named by various names accordingly; they are known *by reason* to be different *masses of qualities*, different objects, which must have been produced by different circumstances. Such variety, therefore, offers no contradiction to our REASON, our EXPECTATIONS, or our TERMS. Yet

Mr. Hume seems to think that nature, without a contradiction to our ideas, may be supposed to alter her course in the *determination of her qualities;* and occasion contrary and different qualities, from otherwise similar objects. Nature, no doubt, preserving in many objects certain appearances to some of the senses, may vary the remaining qualities.

But this cannot be, without her using prevening causes of an altered kind, efficient to the new production; and then it is a new object and must be *newly named.* Such events as these, which are nothing else than all the various events, in the universe, (for all things are *alike* to some of the senses, and *diverse* in others;) nature is full of; but this does not prove, there is not a *necessary connexion* between CAUSE AND EFFECT; and that *custom* only guides our expectations. On the contrary, it is because there can be no " *beginnings* of *existences*" by themselves, that we know, when new phenomena arise, from *apparently* similar circumstances, that we must lie under a mistake; and that the new objects cannot be *the same objects altered*, and elicited from similar circumstances. We might as well deem meteoric stones to be snow, as a body, which had the taste of salt and the feeling of fire. Nature, therefore, cannot, when employing *like* causes in action, alter her course in determining different and contrary "*Effects*" from otherwise similar objects; because in such a case, these *new qualities* would absolutely be *uncaused; different* qualities would be exhibited from *precisely similar conjunctions of bodies*, i. e. *different* and *contrary* qualities, (or Effects) from otherwise similar objects, (or Causes) which is impossible.

Should it be said that nature is supposed to be employing *different* causes in action; by altering the "*secret powers*" (whilst the "*sensible qualities*" remain the same,) that it is in this way she changes her course—then the prevening *conjunctions of bodies* which produced these secret powers, being supposed different; the *natures* of the objects are different; they are truly *other* objects, and there is no astonishment at the production of their altered Effects; *there is no alteration in the course of nature;* and the Phenomena will not support Mr. Hume's argument *against* REASON, and in favour of CUSTOM only; it follows, therefore, that if " we imagine the course of nature *may change,"* it must be under the notion of a *cause equivalent to it:—in which case there is no contradiction offered to the notion of causation as founded on* REASON. But for nature otherwise to change, and to vary either her " *Effects,"* or " *Secret powers,"* without varying the causes or prevening circumstances whose junction formed the objects, whence these result;—is so obviously impossible, that we cannot even suppose the will and power of the Deity to be able to work the *contradiction*. He could not make a finite quality, *dependent* upon himself or some other cause for its exhibition, to become *independent* and able to *exist of itself;* he could not otherwise than by himself altering the determination of the causes that form the objects; then there is a cause for the alleged change—the objects are not *similar* objects; the *whole* prevening circumstances are not the same; and it is only *unlike* causes again that beget *unlike* effects; unlike objects that vary in their qualities.

But the following sentence*, which contains the passage alluded to, involves an ambiguity of expression, which ought to be noticed, lest it should appear as though I had mistaken it, and consequently my answer not appear sufficiently applicable, viz. " Nature may be supposed " to change her course since it implies no " contradiction, that an object SEEMINGLY " like those which we have experienced, " may be attended with different or con- " trary Effects." There is here an ambiguity of sense on account of the expression " SEEMINGLY;" for it may either intend, *an alteration in the determination of Effects from objects, in* ALL OTHER *respects similar, save in these* CONTRARY *effects;* or *an* " ARBITRARY" *change in the* "*secret powers*" "*which* " *mix with the sensible qualities; and on which* " *the effects entirely depend*" in either sense, such an arbitrary change in the course of

---

* Sec. 4. p. 36.

nature, is a "CONTRADICTION TO REASON" and an IMPOSSIBILITY.

Mr. Hume however seems to use it in either of these senses, as the occasion serves, and without conceiving there is much difference between them.

The former sense however appears to be that in which it is used, as applicable in the instance concerning the changes upon snow. Compare these *passages**, " may I not " distinctly conceive, a body *in all other* " *respects* resembling snow having the taste " of salt, and feeling of fire,"—with†, " Every Effect is a distinct event from " its Cause; and ever after it is suggest- " ed, its conjunction must appear *arbi-* " *trary* with its Cause, since there are " always many other effects, which to *rea-* " *son* might seem fully as consistent and " natural." But it is in the latter sense, viz.: in the " *arbitrary*" alteration of the " *secret powers*," (in order to form DIFFERENT

* Essays, Vol. 2. Sec. 4. p. 36.
† Ibid. p. 30.

Causes for the determination of DIFFERENT *Effects*), which must explain the following passage*: " Let the course of nature be allowed hitherto ever so regular proves not that for the future it will continue so." " The secret nature of objects, and consequently all their effects and influences, may change without any change in the sensible qualities;" In either of the senses in which Mr. Hume uses the notion in question, it is equally absurd; for as *Cause* is not by him granted, nature must be supposed to change her regular march *uncaused;* whether in striking off *different* and *contrary* qualities, from objects in *every other* respect similar, *save in these arbitrary and contrary determinations;* or in the mixing *different secret powers* amidst the *sensible qualities.* Nor will it answer for Mr. Hume to shift his position, and say; that the " secret powers" may be considered, as *changed* by the *regular operations of nature;* and that, on account of our inability to detect them,

---

* Ibid. p. 39. The method in which this idea begs the question, has been taken notice of before.

we are necessarily obliged to consider, the *sensible qualities* ONLY, as *like Causes;* thereby concluding the *Effects* will be *similar* upon *insufficient grounds;* and thus REASON, not able to support the idea of a *really* necessary connexion between them.

For upon this supposition, the *real relation* of Cause and Effect, is *assumed as granted*—

1st. In order to account for the change in the secret powers.

2dly. To account for the change in the effects dependent upon them.

And this is at once yielding the whole argument to the adversary*! enabling him justly to retort, that he makes use of the

---

* This sort of argument forms a sophism which logicians term "*ignoratio elenchi;*" "something being proved "which is not necessarily inconsistent with the proposi-"tion maintained:" See W. Logick, p. 240. And this is the real gist, of the whole of Mr. Hume's argument (a *posteriori*) and which is generally considered, I believe, as both acute and *logical*.

general principle concerning Cause and Effect (which is now granted), and which he supports upon "*general reasoning,*" whereby in many instances to *suspect,* and in many others to *detect,* UNlike secret powers amidst the sensible qualities, by which means it becomes applicable, as an AXIOM founded on REASON, wherewith to try every kind of experience both in philosophy and common life—whilst also he can maintain;—that unless it were for the knowledge of such a general principle, *no knowledge* of the " secret powers of nature in ever so many *past* instances, could be of any material service to us *for the future.*

All mathematical demonstration is built upon the notion; that where quantities, or diagrams, resemble each other, the relations which are true, with respect to ONE of each kind will be true with respect to *all* others of a *like* kind; ONLY *because there is nothing else to make a difference among them.* So, if in all *past time,* such *secret powers* could be shown necessarily connected with such *sensible qualities;* yet *in future* it could not thence be proved to continue so, *unless supported by the axioms;—that* LIKE *Causes must* EXHIBIT *like* Effects, *and that* DIFFERENCES CANNOT ARISE *of themselves.*

Upon the whole, therefore, Mr. Hume must be understood to mean, that as we know nothing of " *Cause and Effect,*" or of the "*secret processes of nature,*" so she might be supposed indifferently to strike off contrary Effects from similar prevening Causes, or else to alter their " secret powers," whilst their FORMATION was produced by the same means as usual. Thus that exactly the same circumstances might prevene the falling of snow, (precisely the same objects might unite to produce that object,) upon any two occasions, yet, it might have the taste of salt or feeling of fire ! That the " secret powers of vegetation might in future be altered; although the seasons should roll the same as before; and every power in nature be only equal to the contrary supposition !

To all which I answer, nature cannot alter her course when she is employing *simi-*

lar means in the formation of objects, by changing any of the "Secret powers," or altering any Effects; because the prevening circumstances being supposed in any two cases similar, there would be no assignable reason for the difference. A difference, or change, *either* in the "*secret powers*" of objects, or the *Effects* of Causes, (other things remaining the same) is exactly equal to the CREATION of so *many new qualities*, which could not, without a CONTRADICTION, *arise of themselves.*

I can conceive it said by some, although Mr. Hume would have no right to do so, that a miraculous interference might alter the course of nature; not so, not in determining the production of dissimilar objects from similar causes. No miracle could form an *uncaused* change in nature (which is the notion in question).

A miraculous interference, that is, an interference of God as a cause, might alter the production of objects, yet still there is a *cause* equivalent to the *change*, and again *unlike* objects beget *unlike* qualities: I therefore draw a conclusion from the whole of this reasoning, exactly contrary to Mr. Hume's inference from his; admitting indeed with him, that before experience we cannot know what *particular* effects will flow from given causes; yet *after experience* I judge that it is " *reason* which guides us in " our expectations; because it convinces " us, that instances" (of *Effects,*) " of which " we have had no experience must resem- " ble" (when Causes are similar) " those of " which we have had experience, for that " the course of nature must continue uni- " formly the same," *by the regular determination of like Cause and Effect.*

The same kind of answer will serve for other paradoxical questions which Mr. Hume puts in these Essays.

Is there, says he, any more intelligible proposition than to affirm, that all the trees will flourish in December and January, and decay in May and June? Certainly not, to those who conceive that the " course of nature may without an implied contradiction alter the determination of Effects that proceed from like Causes," or, which is the same thing, exhibit different or contrary qualities, from similar objects. But according to the method I have laid down of viewing the operations of nature, there cannot be a more *unintelligible proposition* than to assert of those trees, which have usually flourished in May and June, that they may cease to do so, and only thrive in December and January.

So far from the mind being able distinctly "*to conceive*" such a change in their qualities, when the proof has been once afforded, that it is their nature to require warmth for their growth; and that cold kills their blossoms; it must be ever after considered impossible for these objects to affect qualities not originally included in their *natures*;—or, for their *natures* to alter, without a cause equivalent to the alteration—or a cause equivalent to it to be *supposed*, without REASON being the foundation of the whole principle of CAUSATION.

To suppose that the circumstances which at first stamped them the objects they are, could enable them to preserve themselves similar objects, and yet arbitrarily put on wholly contrary qualities, seems to be about as reasonable as to assert that black may become white, and white become black, and yet each colour merit its original name, of *black* or *white;* whilst, at the same time, these changes take place on account of such a " change in the course of nature," as determine that although all the causes in action are sufficient only to produce black, yet white shall appear; and *vice versa.* Indeed, before " *nature could be conceived to alter her course;*" the question about which Mr. Hume is *examining experience* (namely, whether she will support the knowledge of the necessary connexion of like objects and their qualities,) must be supposed to be *already* answered in the *negative;* and that it is KNOWN *that nature may be supposed* to exhibit *similar* antecedents *followed* by *different* subsequents, or in other words that there is *no necessary connexion* between like objects and like qualities; which is begging the question; and in a different way from that in which he means to answer it, for he means to support the doctrine of necessary connexion, though upon principles peculiarly his own. Should it be said that I assume the contrary position, I answer, I do not *assume* it; but have previously proved the general conclusion, that " all like causes must have like effects; (because otherwise, *objects would begin of themselves:*) in order purposely to show that " nature cannot alter her course." Mr. Hume makes also a great mistake in supposing because we can conceive in the fancy the existence of objects contrary to our experience, that therefore they may really exist in nature; for it by no means follows that things which are incongruous in nature, may not be contemplated by the imagination, and received as possible until reason shows the contrary. Indeed, the fallacy, on which his whole sceptical doctrines are *built*, may be seen at the very outset of his first Essay. He imagines it impossible to conceive the *contrary* to any *known relation* in quantities; but that we may *conceive* the *contrary of every matter of fact as possible*—impossible, under *the same circumstances*, and if the *circumstances alter*, the fact is a *different fact;* but not a *contrary one*—any more than the *different* relations of various quantities are not *contrary* to each other. Mr. Hume did not perceive that all objects whatever in relation to us, are but masses of certain qualities elicited from certain prevening circumstances, and therefore incapable of having different qualities, (or of showing diverse effects) whilst yet they remain similar objects *born under like circumstances.* He did not perceive that the " *productive principle,*" or *the Cause of an Effect,* is to be found *in the junction of objects already existing,* by which new objects are formed; but conceiving the nature of the operation of this principle to be wholly unknown, he imagined and alleged all things to be only " *conjoined,* and *not connected;*" and that they might change their places fortuitously; custom only connecting them in the fancy; and a contrary fancy as capable of unconnecting them again.

Strange philosophy! " Effects may be supposed non-existent this minute, and existent the next;" (and so in suspense,) and may therefore " begin their existence by themselves."—If this be so, undoubtedly we want no Causes for our Effects; our Rose-trees may suspend their blossoms in June; the flower require no warmth for its expansion, and remain non-existent till December!

That different objects have different qualities, all are well acquainted with;—The Chinese rose, and the holley, can thrive in Winter; but the same kind of rose, that hitherto has grown only in spring, and flourished in summer, can no more put forth its leaves and expand its blossoms in winter, than the mercury in a *tried* thermometer can suddenly contract to the freezing point, in a burning summer's day.

Let us however, before quitting this important and interesting argument, chuse an example to prove, that " nature cannot without a contradiction be imagined to alter her course." Let a receiver be imagined void of every substance whatever; and nothing but an *uncoloured space* within it. Now it is surely the " course of nature," for this uncoloured space to *remain as it is*, without some *cause steps in to alter it;* and if *some cause steps in to alter it,* "nature does *not* alter her course." Then let nature be supposed to alter her course, and a *scarlet colour uncaused* to enter. Does not every reader perceive the impossibility that scarlet uncaused could enter? that it could " start of itself into existence?" yet such is the idea that is veiled under Mr. Hume's argument;—that different and contrary qualities can take place in similar circumstances; that a rose may blow in winter, when the causes were efficient to its blowing only in June! No circumstances are supposed changed; and yet " *of itself,*" the nature of the rose may change!—and so may a new phenomenon take place in an *empty receiver*, as the entrance of a scarlet colour, or of a dove, or any other imaginable being, without an equivalent change of circumstances for its introduction.

The sum of Mr. Hume's argument is, that we knowing nothing of the " secrets of nature," we cannot know there is really a necessary connexion between objects; but *imagining* there is, this *imagination* arises, from a CUSTOMARY OBSERVATION, of *the invariableness of their antecedence and subsequence;*—which invariableness, however, does not prove, that each connexion may be more than an *insulated casual event;* not obligatory in nature; therefore *other subsequent* events might, without a contradiction, be imagined to happen after *similar antecedents*, and a *different order of events* might be supposed in the " course of nature."

Now shortly the whole of this reasoning concerning the *possibility of nature altering her course*, is but a circle! for the argument is invented to show that CUSTOM *not* REASON, must be the only ground of our belief in the relation of Cause and Effect.—But it is *impossible to imagine such a change in nature,* unless *reason* were previously excluded as the principle of that relation;—*and it is impossible to exclude reason as the principle of that relation*, except by supposing *that nature may alter her course.*—Thus the idea of *causation*, is founded only on *experience**, ex-

---

* " The opinion that a cause is necessary to every
" new production arises from experience."—TREATISE.

perience is supplied with arguments by *custom* not by *reason* * and custom is supported in her authority by a supposed change in nature †, *impossible* to any idea of causation ‡, *unless* ALREADY SUPPOSED TO BE MERELY THE EFFECT OF CUSTOM §.

Nor must we conclude this branch of the subject, without observing the contradiction that lies in the very endeavour to persuade the world that *custom is the true* " CAUSE *of* BELIEF" *in necessary connexion*, when before assenting to such a doctrine it must give up all usual habits of thinking upon the subject, and believe upon Mr.

---

* " All inferences from experience are Effects of *cus-*
" *tom* not of *reasoning.*"—ESSAYS.

† " Since it implies no contradiction that the course
" of nature may change, there can be no demonstrative
" arguments in the case."—ESSAYS.
" Wherever there is a propensity without being
" impelled by any reasoning we say this propensity is the
" *Effect* of custom."—ESSAYS.

‡ " If *there* were nothing to bind objects together the
" inferences from present facts would be entirely precari-
" ous."—ESSAYS.

§ " Our belief in *causation* is the Effect of custom."—
ESSAYS.

Hume's reasoning, what it never before believed!—

Mr. Hume himself recapitulates his argument thus:

" Every idea is copied from some preceding impression (idea being an Effect *derived* from impression as its Cause). In all single instances of the operation of bodies there is nothing that produces, nor consequently can suggest the idea of necessary connexion. But when *many* instances appear, we *feel* a new impression, a customary connexion in the thought, between one object and its usual attendant*."

Now this method of placing the argument is but the statement of *another circle*; for *causation* is used as the very principle which lies at the foundation of

---

* Compare the Treatise and Essays,—in both works *impressions* are considered as absolutely necessary to *cause* ideas—to create them;—to *produce* them;—they are considered as the truly " productive principle" of ideas—Objects without which they could not exist.

the whole system; and afterwards we are desired to search for the *impression*, which is the CAUSE of that EFFECT, viz. the *idea causation*.

And it is no answer to say that the notion of causation is spoken of in his own sense, not in his adversary's; for in either sense it is equally illogical, to prove the conclusion by the premises, and the premises by the conclusion.

What should we think of an author, who, in attempting to account for the original discovery of metals, proved that it was effected by the use of instruments framed from a material termed *iron*, drawn from the bowels of the earth?

In like manner there is *a want of logical precision* in referring all the principles which connect our ideas to three kinds of associations amongst them; of which *causation* is ranked as one;—and then (in order to account for causation,) shew the power that lies in the associations of ideas. Such a notion ends in the formation of a mere identical proposition; *viz.* a certain association of ideas is causation; and causation consists in an association of ideas.

But there is still another passage in Mr. Hume's Essays, of greater consequence than any I have quoted, or argued on; and which I shall yet detain the reader for a few moments in order to consider; it is this following:

"As reason is incapable of any va-
"riation, the conclusions which it draws
"from one circle, are the same which
"it would form from surveying all the
"circles in the universe. But no man
"having seen one body move after being
"impelled by another would infer, that
"*every body* will move after a like im-
"pulse*."

This passage I consider as containing the whole gist of Mr. Hume's error, and therefore it points out where my answer should meet it. The error consists, in mak-

* Essays, Vol. 2. Sec. 5, p. 47.

ing an *incomplete comparison*, between the two subjects compared. *Every body* is taken in an indefinite sense for every *kind of body;* but *circle* is not taken for every *kind of figure.* The reason whence the CONCLUSIONS concerning all circles are *general,* is upon the very principle of Cause and Effect; for I know by experience, that upon the first study of Mathematical science, I found much difficulty in a philosophical objection I could not easily answer; namely; that the relations of the quantities in one figure did not seem *necessarily* applicable to *all* of a like kind; until I perceived that the affections of *all*, were INVOLVED in *one* of *each kind;* as there was nothing to occasion a *difference* amidst their relations. Now then let the data be the same, and the IMPULSE *given* not only be *like*, but the BODY *given be like;* and I conceive that every man, and every child, would expect, upon a second trial, that the same body would move in the same manner as before. The inference would be drawn from the mind perceiving, (in the first instance,) that no motion would have taken place except from the conjunction of the body with the impulsive force; and in the second case would add to the memory of this Effect, the reasoning, that there being nothing else to make a difference, a like Effect would again take place. Nay, I am persuaded, that reason might go so far as, from calculating the proportions of the impulse used, and the body moved, to conclude the varieties, which would take place under proportionably different circumstances.

Mr. Hume draws two inferences of much consequence from his doctrine; 1st, that as our *custom of thinking* is not the *operation of nature*, so we have no positive proof, that a cause is wanted for the existence of the universe as of a *truly " productive principle."* 2dly, That it is *unreasonable to believe in miracles*, because it is foolish to allow of our *customary habits of thinking*, which arise from " experience in the course of nature," to be interfered with by an " *experience of a less frequent occurrence;*" which dependence upon testimony can only afford. This latter inference he professes in his Essay against Miracles. The former opinion is less openly acknowledged; not being stated in explicit terms, but of immediate inference from the doctrine; and which he was well aware of, was the case.

The sum of my answer and argument is, that although we know not the "secrets of nature," yet we know that nothing can "begin its own existence;" therefore there must truly be a "productive principle," a cause necessary for every new existence in nature;—that we gain the knowledge of a "necessary connexion between Cause and Effect," by an *experimentum crucis*, and therefore no greater number of invariable antecedents and consequents are wanted, than what is necessary, in order *to observe* what circumstances *affect* each other, or the contrary. That neither *fancy* nor *custom* creates the notion by an association of ideas; but the UNDERSTANDING gains it, by an observation of what is *that circumstance, without which a new object does not exist.* Things therefore could not change their places, nor nature alter her course, without a contradiction.

Hence it is that a cause is wanted in the universe equivalent to the change from non-existence to existence! And also that it is not more unreasonable to believe in miracles than in any other extraordinary phenomena in nature, when we may suppose, that *efficient Causes have been in action*, towards their production; and that *final causes* are of *sufficient weight to justify the altered work of Providence!*

But a minute investigation of Mr. Hume's Essay on Miracles is much wanted. The purport of it, and the method by which it is drawn out as a consequence from the three preceding Essays, has not (that I know of) been observed by the learned. One would think at first sight that Mr. Hume, in admitting that the " course of nature might change," conceded much to the Christians. Instead of which he adroitly turns round upon them, and says, " so it may in fact;" but in " custom" you *think it cannot*, therefore it is absurd to allow this custom of thought to be overthrown by testimony. In this struggle of fancy, against fancy, the more powerful must and ought to prevail!— If these pages should find favour before the public, an examination of the Essay on Miracles is intended to follow them; without which the answer to these on Cause and Effect is hardly complete.

Should an objection arise to my doctrine, that on account of supposing causes to act as the junctions of different qualities, and yet by pushing back all causes to the ONE UNCAUSED ESSENCE; I thereby prevent the idea of him being reposed in as a Cause; as he forms ONE object only: I answer, that the uncaused essence, however mysterious in his nature, and however awful and distant to our speculations, must nevertheless have attributes; or in other words, its own peculiar qualities, which required no former beings, to *give birth to them.*

The unions of such qualities among themselves, might well be equal to the going forth of the great Creation! The union of *wisdom*, with benevolence; and of these with the "*power*" arising out of the inexhaustible resources of his essence, might well occasion the " starting forth" of innumerable beings; the highest orders of which, without the slightest philosophical contradiction, might be considered as coeval and coequal with the Father " as touching the Godhead." But after this, the wide universe, with all its gradations of wonderful beings, with all its powers of life and heat, and motion, must have come out from him according to the laws with which they were endowed. And although the original undivided essence, whose qualities were equal to such creation, must be considered as antecedent to his own work; yet the *operation* of that essence must ever have been the same from all eternity; and in that point of view, the *junction* of wisdom and benevolence, with whatever " *capacities*" of that essence were efficient to their ends, must have been accompanied with their instant synchronous Effects;—the *formation of inferior beings.* " Let there be light," said God, " and there was light."

Thus God, the universal Father, and with him any noble *manifestations* of his essence; then archangel, and angel; man (or beings analogous to him) and animals; mind, and matter; may be considered as having existed eternally, coming forth from him, living in him, and supported by him; whilst an analogous state of being must be expected to continue eternally, in like manner—and it may also be expected as a circumstance consistent and probable with the whole of so grand an arrangement, that some inferior orders of beings may be raised in the scale of nature, to be inhabitants of a kindlier world than this; with enlarged capacities for happiness and virtue.

The consideration of the method the understanding has recourse to, in order to judge of the probable presence of similar causes on the contrary, will come under our view in the next Chapter.

CHAPTER THE THIRD.

I shall now proceed to apply the principles already laid down, to the examination of the question concerning the guidance of our expectations in ordinary life, which question forms the subject of the Essay entitled Sceptical Doubts concerning the operations of the Understanding. The question itself might be shortly stated thus:—why does the operation of the apparent qualities of an object upon the senses, lead the mind to expect the action of its untried qualities, when placed in fit circumstances for their operation?

Why should bread, on account of its formerly nourishing the body, be expected to nourish it again? why may it not, whilst it preserves " its colour, consistence, &c." nevertheless destroy the human frame?

In my answer to these questions, I shall allow to Mr. Hume, that the memory of the sensible and *apparent* qualities of any object, is necessary to the acknowledgment of it as the same body, upon every acquaintance with it; also that the *memory of what its qualities will be*, when conjoined with any other, is also requisite to the *expectation* of any farther qualities arising from it.

The idea of these must be associated with the sensible qualities; but the knowledge that they will assuredly take place, when existing in like circumstances, is founded upon much stronger principles than those of custom and habit.

It is founded—

First,—Upon a quick, steady, accurate observation, *whether the prevening causes are the* SAME, *from which an object is elicited in any* PRESENT *instance, as upon a* FORMER *one;*—and,

2dly,—Upon a demonstration, that if the observation hath been correct, the result—(i. e. the *whole* effects or qualities,) must necessarily be the same as heretofore;

otherwise contrary qualities, as already discussed, would arise without a cause, i. e. a *difference begin of itself*, which has been shown to be impossible*. Thus the first step the mind takes, in order to be satisfied that the same *apparent qualities* in any object will be attended with like " *secret powers,*" is the consideration, from the surrounding circumstances, of what the prevening causes were, which gave *birth to the object;* and therefore whether the *apparent qualities* are *truly* the accompaniments of the *same nature* or not.—As for instance, we can form a notion almost with certainty, whether the substance placed upon the table has been truly elicited from such causes, as could alone produce the compound object bread. Whether the pure liquid offered, be the result of such circum-

---

* It has already been shown upon mathematical principles, that a *difference* in the *result* of equal unions, can no more arise out of the *mixtures of any other qualities of objects,* than from the *junctions of those of number*. If ONE added to ONE, bear out the result TWO, *once;* it must ever do so; and if a certain proportion of *blue and yellow particles,* form a mixture termed GREEN, *once;* GREEN in like manner shall ever *thence* result.

stances as render it water, or of such others, as may prove it, (notwithstanding its apparent quality to the eye,) to be spirits of ammonia? &c. It is not the *mere* appearance of the external qualities, which can determine the mind to expect certain effects; it is only that *appearance in conjunction with the recollection of the probable causes, that have produced the objects in question*, and which lead the mind to suppose the said objects to be truly bread, water, or hartshorn; and therefore impossible not to be capable of exhibiting all their qualities, and none other than their qualities.

The first step belongs to those combined qualities of mind called good sense; and will always be made with an assurance and propriety in proportion to it. The nature of its operation is this;—the mind knows that different objects have the same apparent qualities to some of the senses, which cannot afford a sufficient test concerning the farther exhibition of others;— but observation enables it to judge, when an object is presented, what *causes have been used in its formation;* and if it perceives that the causes have been similar, it *knows* that the whole effects or qualities must necessarily be similar; otherwise there might be an uncaused " change in the course of nature;" which, although sometimes *philosophers* imagine possible, *no ordinary minds* ever do, because they never think a *change* can take place of itself; or in other words, qualities begin their own existences

It is nothing but this reasoning concerning the *causes*, used in the *formation of an object*, which makes us argue to the " secret powers," and the similar appearances only guide us, in as far as they form a proof that they are truly the same objects, with respect to those appearances; for SIMILAR *objects* could not have *different appearances.*

The way to try the case is to observe the action of the mind, when two objects are presented of precisely similar appearance, but which may be thought, on account of the uncertainty as to the circumstances which excited them, possibly, to possess different properties.

We always enquire, in such cases, as to some *leading circumstance*, which may enable us to judge what causes were used in their formation.

If an ignorant person, for instance, whom we perceived could not read, were about to serve us in a chymist's shop with *Epsom salts;* we, being aware that *oxalic acid* had the same *apparent* qualities, should not feel an assurance in the " *secret powers;*" but would cautiously enquire for some mark, by which to be guided in our notion as to their *original* FORMATION;—i. e. as to what mass of qualities *apparent*, and *secret*, had been combined by the hand of nature, or art, in the object before us. It is here that Mr. Hume's mistake is evident in the statement of what he deems an irresolvable difficulty, concerning the method of the mind in the *guidance* of its expectation with respect to the *untried qualities*, or "Effects," of the objects presented to it.

These are his words,—

"The two following propositions are far from being the same; I have found that such an object has always been attended with such an Effect; and I foresee that all other objects, in *appearance similar*, will be attended with similar effects." The connexion between the two propositions is not intuitive; of what nature is it then? I answer, WE NEVER DO MAKE THE CONNEXION—*we never do foresee that objects similar in appearance* ONLY, will be attended with *similar Effects.*— But as *truly similar* objects, must necessarily *appear* the same, we combine these acknowledged similarities, with the circumstances which we are aware of, as *most probable to have been used in their formation*, and thence judge whether the object be *truly* a mass of similar Effects or qualities, elicited from like causes in action, or the contrary.

If the causes in action have been the same; (and we are pretty good judges if they have, or have not, in the vast variety of ordinary cases with which we have to do,) then the objects in question must necessarily possess the whole qualities which belong to their natures, whether taken *singly*, and acting *alone* on the senses; or acting in *conjunction with another object*, and exhibiting those *further qualities*, which are usually termed " *Effects.*"

Thus Mr. Hume's statement—" I have " found such an object has always been at- " tended with such an effect; and I foresee " other objects, in *appearance* similar, will " be attended with similar effects;" is not the state of the human mind in any given circumstance. It should rather run thus, (although the familiarity we have from infancy with the objects of life prevent the notion from being so distinctly formed, much less expressed, as to be easily detected when called upon.)

Here is an object which has been the result of LIKE CAUSES IN ACTION, *now* as *formerly*. The *whole* mass of Effects, which *those causes once* produced, must necessarily *be again* capable of being exhibited in like appropriate circumstances.

It may also be added, that when an object in nature is, on account of some governing circumstance relating to it, considered as a similar object with another; because that governing circumstance points out the creating causes of it; then the " Effects," as well as the *apparent* qualities, enter into its definition, and *bread* stands as a sign of *all the ideas under the term*, and of *nothing but the ideas*.

It receives that name on account of its *tried qualities*, and it retains it, when *known to have been formed by those creating causes*, that necessarily can only determine *similar effects*.

If the human body is in the same state on any occasion, as on that when bread nourished it; there is as great a necessity it should again *nourish*, as that it should be *white*.

Thus all experimental reasoning consists in an *observation*, and a *demonstration*, as has before been shown;—an *observation*, whether the circumstances from which an object is produced, and in which it is placed, are the same upon one occasion as upon another;—and a *demonstration*, that if it is so, *all its exhibitions will be the same.* But Mr. Hume asks in another question of the same nature, why we judge *otherwise* concerning the "Effects," (or untried qualities), following the apparent qualities, in some other objects.

"Nothing, says he, so like as eggs; "yet no one, on account of this apparent "similarity, expects the same taste and "relish in all of them;" "Now where is "that process of reasoning, which from one "instance, draws a conclusion so different "from that which it infers from a hundred "others?"

The reason is, because it is one of the *tried, known, qualities* of eggs, to become soon changed in their flavour; without any great indication of such change becoming apparent to the eye;—therefore again, there is *not* a connexion between the apparent qualities, and " secret powers," and we should enquire if *we doubted;* concerning *some circumstance before tasting* that might afford *a discreet judgment*, some ground for conceiving that *only* those causes, had hitherto been in action, which had been likely to produce *fresh eggs.*

This instance forms an argument on my side of the question, rather than on Mr. Hume's; as it shows there is not an absolute connexion, (and that the mind never thinks there is,) between *the mere* APPEARANCES, and the " *Effects*" *of an object;*— but that we judge concerning the probability of the method in which an object has been *formed*, and of *the circumstances it may have been placed in afterwards, as likely or not to alter it;* before we announce, whether the *apparent* qualities are indications of those " *secret powers, on which the Effects entirely depend."*

Thus I not only assert, that *these are*

"the steps" the mind takes, from *experiment* to *expectation;* namely, ONE OF A HIGH PROBABILITY, that the prevening circumstances which determine those *masses of Effects,* (or qualities) called *objects,* have rendered them *the same* upon a present occasion, as upon a past; AND ONE OF DEMONSTRATION, that IF they are the same objects, *all* the *unexhibited* qualities, or *effects,* must also be THE SAME; but I also affirm, that " *custom*" is not, cannot, be the principle on which the notion of necessary connexion between Cause and Effect is really founded; and that with respect to the most familiar objects of our life it has only a partial operation, in governing our expectations of the future. I grant that custom or an association of ideas, arising from those habits which infix ideas in the mind, is the foundation of all *memory;* and therefore similar appearances, suggest the *remembered unexhibited accompanying qualities* of objects; but it will not suit *all* the phenomena; it will not give the *assurance* that the accompanying untried qualities, must of necessity take place; and that the object in question merits the name assigned to it. In order to prove this proposition, let us try any of the various strongly associated circumstances, which govern the mind, where clearly the suggestion to the imagination, can arise from nothing else but association of ideas. The ideas of these may always be disjoined from each other, without any apparent inconceivableness to the fancy; which is always the case in endeavouring to imagine a *similar cause* to take place with *one we have before known*, and a *different Effect* follow, from *that* which had *previously followed it*.

Let any school-boy, who always joins the first two lines in Virgil together, endeavour to imagine one line only written, without the other; he can do it; or that Virgil might have made another line, the first remaining the same; he can; one is not the *cause* of the other; nor, are they necessarily connected. But when he says, twice 2 are 4, he finds that the consequence of two units being taken two times over, necessarily exhibit four units to the mind; and cannot be disjoined from that result, while the terms are spoken of in the same sense.

Like Causes necessarily *include*, and therefore *produce* and *exhibit* their *Effects*. The mind indeed may be forced from every recollection of habit, and consider the qualities of an object apart from each other, as in any other association: but the mind never can consider them as *possible* to exist *apart in nature;* it never for a moment supposes it but *inconceivable*, and impossible, that they should be " non-existent this moment, and " existent the next" without conjoining to them the idea of a cause or " productive principle."

The only difficulty the mind has to do with, in forming a right judgment concerning its expectations of the qualities of objects, is the probability, or the contrary, whether the circumstances which formed them, are the same as heretofore or not.—But this part of the question, we always consider with more or less nicety of induction; and do not believe them to be so, from external appearances only, but from those circumstances which enable us to know, what *course nature was taking, when she stamped them such as we see them.*

We judge in short that nature, in the continuance of her plan, is constant still to her own great ends; where the first beginnings of the work are wholly out of our cognizance.

We judge from the memory, of the parts we have ourselves taken in the disposition of Causes.

We judge from the knowledge we have had of the actions of others, and of the parts they have also been performing in their disposition; and when these are all in the affirmative, towards the probability of like Causes having been in action, in the formation of any object immediately concerning us; then we judge that the similar appearances, are qualities, of a like object, which only remains to be tried, to justify the assumption that *it is the same;* and that it deserves *the name* which has been bestowed on it accordingly. I think this answers the whole argument, and is sufficient to prove, that " *reason*" not " *custom*" is the great guide of human life; convincing us, that the " instances of which we have had no experience, must resemble those of which we have had experience, for that the course of nature must continue uniformly the same."

SECTION THE SECOND.

In the course of writing these pages, I have met with some passages in the works of Mr. Locke, which when compared with the whole of Mr. Hume's argument, (*à posteriori,*) must be considered as forming the basis of that elaborate and inconclusive reasoning. Mr. Locke says, " there is a " supposition that *nature works regularly* " in the production of things, and sets the " boundaries to each species;—whereas " any one who observes their different qua" lities, can hardly doubt that many of the " individuals called by the same name, are " in their *internal constitution* different from " one another."

Again; "Let the complex idea of gold, be made up of whatever other qualities you please, malleableness will not appear to depend on that complex idea. The connexion that malleableness has with those other qualities, being only by the intervention of the real collection of its insensible parts; which since we know not, it is impossible we should perceive that connection, &c."

In another place he has; "But we are so far from being admitted into the *secrets of nature*, that we scarce so much as ever approach the first step towards them."

The parallel passages in Mr. Hume's writings I need not again quote, especially as, if the reader has been interested in the course of this discussion, they will immediately recur to his memory.

Now Mr. Locke never meant to say that the differences of species could take place, excepting by the *regular operations* of CAUSES, *necessarily connected with their* EFFECTS; for he considered the sensible qualities of bodies, as dependant upon their internal constitution; which is both to acknowledge the relation of Cause and Effect, as also to conceive the *sensible qualities,* to be the EFFECTS of the *secret powers**.

Both of these principles Mr. Hume denies; saying expressly of the latter—" It " is acknowledged on all hands, there is " no connection between the sensible qua-" lities, and those secret powers of objects, " on which the effects entirely depend."— Which latter remark I consider not only as erroneous, but astonishing! in as much as the ideas in this part of his Essay, are an obvious expansion of those of Mr. Locke, who is an *exception* to the notion of an universal agreement to this opinion; (being *one*, at least, and in authority equal to many, who does not acknowledge it.) The doubt however which Mr. Locke throws out, although it does in no respect affect the general prin-

---

* " That every thing has a real constitution, whereby it " is, what it is, and on which its sensible qualities depend, " is past doubt."—Locke's Essay on the Human Understanding.

ciples concerning causation; yet it regards the difficulty there is in the *detection* of like objects, on account of our inability to form a judgment concerning their *internal constitutions*, from the *mere appearance* of their sensible qualities.

I consider Mr. Locke renders the difficulty something greater than it need be; although he acknowledges that a similarity in the sensible qualities forms an argument of high probability, (though short of demonstration,) in favor of the presence of truly similar objects.

For as the secret, external, unknown powers or qualities, in nature; determine the sensible qualities as their *effects*, as well as every other effect, or property; so when we perceive the sensible qualities in any instances to be *like*, we know that *as far as they go*, they are LIKE *Effects*, from like SECRET *constitutions;* which *secret constitutions* having been once able to determine certain effects, may do the same again; and not only *may*, but *must* do so again, *unless something has* occurred unobserved to make a difference among them.

In order to form a judgment if any thing is likely to have occurred towards making such an *alteration;* the mind has recourse to several observations and reasonings.—For considering that a certain figured, limited, portion of extended matter in nature, does by the action of the *self same particles,* exhibit different qualities, according to the different senses they meet, or variety of objects, with which they mix; so it applies these masses to the examination of more senses than one, for an higher certainty in this matter; knowing it to be very rare, but that a diversity is detected among the particles, by some *one* sense, at least. The senses, therefore, are considered capable of *nearly* detecting the similarity of internal constitutions; and this upon such a *regularity in fact* of the course of nature, which must itself be looked upon as a general Effect, from a general Cause.

Nevertheless the proposition founded on these trials, is but a probability, although a high one.

But, 2dly. The mind has always a regard to the *method* taken by *nature* and *art* in the FORMATION of an object. When these are similar; the MASSES of *Effects*, or *objects*, are necessarily similar; and SUCH therefore will be *their* Effects in *their turn.* Then these *forming objects* are still silently traced backwards; in order to perceive if their production hath been similar—till we rest at last in those grand objects and operations in nature, which we have found so universally regular to certain ends, that upon the *general relation* of Cause and Effect, (as applicable to this particular case,) we *conclude*, that such a *regular like Effect*, can only be the result of a *like* continual cause; which shall not alter as long as the GREAT FIRST CAUSE doth not alter his pleasure therein. Thus we trace the *sensible qualities* of bread to the SECRET CONSTITUTIONS which have partly been put in action, by the sower and reaper of corn, the operations of the miller and the baker; and beyond these to the influence of the air, the sun, and the juices of the earth; which objects as they originally seem to have "come forth from the Father of man" for his use, so have they ever continued too true to their destination, not to be considered as dependant on that "God of seasons," who has ordained the nourishment of his children to arise from "*bread, earned by the sweat of their brow.*"

It is, on account of these reasons, (that in answer to Mr. Hume) I say, that "other bread will also nourish, when a body of a like colour and consistency has frequently done so; and which remains free from the suspicion of any other beings having been concerned in its FORMATION than those alluded to. *Frequency of repetition*, abstracted from the *principle of* CAUSATION *as a* CONCLUSION *already drawn* from "*general reasoning,*" is not a circumstance sufficient to generate such a principle, either from *custom*, or aught else; but being previously known and believed in; *frequency of repetition* becomes legitimately to be considered as an *Effect*, from a *Cause*, equally constant and general in its exhibition; and thereby begets a *reasonable*, as well as a customary dependance, upon the *necessary connexion*, that is between such regular Cause and Effect.

Thus the most ignorant conceive; *first* that qualities cannot begin of themselves; for there is as quick and accurate a perception, of natural contradictions in terms, amidst the least as the most learned of men: they therefore believe in *Cause*, as a " productive principle" in general. Secondly, they believe that regularity in nature is an Effect whose *Cause* they may regularly depend on, as a corollary with the preceding principle. Thirdly, they believe there is the intimate connexion of Cause and Effect between the secret powers, and sensible qualities of objects; conceiving that an OUTWARD *indefinite object*, which when it meets with the eye presents to it a certain colour, and with the touch a certain consistency, and which they believe to be FORMED from certain materials, will *also*, upon trial, be palateable to the taste, agreeable to the stomach, and nourishing to the body.

Thus when Mr. Hume says, " I require *for my information* what reasoning it is that leads men, from the mere sensible qualities of things to expect their future Effects?" he requires the statement of an argument, which in fact is never made; for men conceive that it is *something indefinite*; i. e. a certain mass of particles determined into that mass by forming powers equivalent to it, which meeting with the eyes, is seen of a defined colour, with the touch yields the sense of a certain consistency, and when entering the stomach shall be enjoyed as a satisfaction to hunger*. *None ever suppose*, that it is what is *first* seen and felt—that it is *colour and consistency* which *afterwards* NOURISHES.—*They suppose it is that which is sown and reaped, and kneaded and baked;* which seen, or *unseen;* touched or *untouched;* is FITTED TO NOURISH; but being seen, shall be white or brown; and being felt, shall be of a less or greater

* This part of the subject again touches upon the Berkleyan theory, concerning external nature; and the opinions ordinary minds have of the *external existence*, or the contrary, of the sensible qualities: upon *which point* Hume and Berkeley are at variance.

compressibility. The *sensible* qualities are only considered as SIGNS of the secret powers,—which *secret powers* are understood to be determined by certain similar processes of *art*, mixed with the grand and regular operations of nature. When the *formation* of objects can be less accurately detected; their similarity of internal constitution becomes more doubtful, from the mere appearance of *some* of the sensible qualities only;—for, the greater number of qualities which are exhibited as similar to the senses, the higher does the proof become, of the secret powers being also similar.

Fourthly.—The mind, (of ordinary persons especially), though appearing to reason upon this subject in a *circle*, yet in reality escapes the sophism and proceeds by a method involving much practical result and rational evidence. For instance; if there were an *appearance* of fire, doubted, as to its being more than a *mere* appearance of it;—the moment it were known to have been elicited from the concussion of flint and steel, there would no longer be a doubt on that matter. Then if in any case did the question arise, whether those objects usually considered as *flint and steel*, were truly such, it would be thought a proof in the affirmative, if upon their concussion they could elicit a *sensible* spark. Philosophers might imagine the *secret powers* of the *whole* to be altered; but plain understandings would consider the *entire coincidence* to be too great and remarkable to arise from *chance*. Such *sensible causes*, giving birth to such *sensible effects*, they would suppose formed a connection of the highest probability, whence to form a judgment, that the whole secret powers of each were similar. And in cases of high probability the mind is as much *determined* to action, as by demonstration. It cannot stand hesitating, and therefore " takes a step," (in arguing from the sensible qualities to the future effects of things,) governed by a *high probability* founded on REASONING " that *they* ARE" connected with like secret *powers, on which the Effects entirely depend.*

Nor is this argument in a circle, for the mind does not reason from the Effects to the Causes; and from the Causes back again to the Effects, but considers in each of these cases, that the *invariable regularity* of nature is a POWER that may be depended upon; and from which fact of *invariableness* the reasonable argument is framed, that the same secret powers will accompany the sensible qualities which have ever done so, when elicited from like *apparent Causes*. It is an additional proof added to the APPEARANCE *of fire*, that it is REALLY such, if found to be the result not only of *apparently* like Causes in action, but of such that have *never been known to* MISS FIRE, when they have *seemed* to kindle it. Whilst should the temper of steel lie under any suspicion, of incapacity as to the determination of its Effects; if upon trial, the spark be immediately emitted, the conclusion is as immediate that this Effect is similar in the secret powers, which nature in no instance ever failed, to determine along with such sensible qualities.

In moral feelings also, I might argue that had I a friend whose absence might suggest a dread, lest the *powers* of his friendship had become weakened; if upon his return I observed the same *sensible manifestations* of regard as heretofore I should have very reasonable ground to judge, that they were the symptoms of a *heart*, as true to me as ever, whose faith was always found to shew itself *in similar demonstrations of kindness.*

It is one of the most ordinary modes of reasoning that the generality of mankind possess; to consider invariability of recurrence as incapable of arising from *chance.*—The meaning of which is, that having the principle of general causation already in their minds, they judge that invariable regularity cannot be *undesigned* and without an end in view, (as well as that it is itself an *Effect*, and must therefore have its own Cause, i. e. a *regular* invariable Cause of whose very *essence* it is, only to determine similar Effects.) And it is remarkable that this idea and in the *very same language* expressing it, is used at the beginning of Mr. Hume's "*Treatise*," as the sole foundation of a system expressly undertaken to prove that the mind never *reasons*, from experience to expectation. His words are to this purpose; "*this coincidence,*" (viz. of an IDEA always requiring an IMPRESSION to prevene it,) "IS TOO GREAT TO ARISE FROM CHANCE!"

To return to Mr. Locke, he merely meant to say, that nature in her regular and usual modes of operation, from Cause and Effect might form *irregular collections of qualities*, not to be detected by mere appearances; and therefore unworthy *on that account only*, of retaining the *names* of regular species, which are *also named* on account of their *tried* Effects and properties. But every man acquainted with Mr. Locke's writings must consider him, as far from wishing to authorize in future times such a scheme as that of Mr. Hume's. Nor do I think he would dissent from my notions, that the method the mind takes to judge of the kind of objects which are present, is:

1stly.—By tracing the *manner* of their formation.

2dly.—By considering an invariable regularity in nature as reasonable to be depended upon, being itself an invariable effect from an equal Cause.

3dly.—By the application of various senses to the affections of the particles.

4thly.—By the consideration that the sensible qualities being similar is a presumption in favor of similar secret powers, as *truly* similar objects would necessarily *appear* the same.

5thly.—That in like manner when *Effects* are *apparently* similar a presumption is formed in favor of apparently similar causes, having given birth to *like secret powers* in the EFFECTS, as well as *their sensible qualities*.

6thly.—That the mind quickly and habitually surveys these things; so that the understanding being *accomplished* in such latent, and constant reasoning; may uniformly blend and use it, although it may find a difficulty of analyzing it when called for.

7thly.—That after the application of an exact experiment, it is imposible to imagine a difference of qualities to arise under the same circumstances.

It is strange that a system at once so unstable and confused, as Mr. Hume's, should ever have been built upon any notions of Mr. Locke, whose moral conclusions are so much at variance with his. Divest Mr. Hume's ideas of the air, of science and grace, which he throws around them, and present them in a plain and popular manner, they will appear thus.—" The mind cannot become acquainted with the knowledge of a necessary connexion between Cause and Effect; for there exists no relations amidst things, of which an *idea* can be conveyed to it, except by the means of an original *impression*."

" But in nature events are entirely *unconnected*, therefore not capable of conveying an *impression* of *necessary connexion*, or of POWER; yet men conceive that events, are *not thus unconnected*—in which idea they are mistaken; as *experience*, which is the ONLY field for their observation in this matter, merely offers to view certain similar sensible qualities, which are *frequently*, although not *invariably* followed by other similar sensible qualities. In certain cases, however, there have been such *invariable* sequences (though " of *loose, casual, unconnected events*") that a definition of Cause and Effect, as of an *invariable* sequence, may be *framed thereon*."

" In as much as it is only like sensible qualities with which we are acquainted, so they alone are considered as like *Causes* or *antecedents;* and they have *no connexion* with the *secret powers of objects*,—which secret powers, are *nevertheless the only true Causes on* " *which the Effects entirely depend;*—therefore *like* sensible qualities NOT being like Causes might be followed by *different* Effects."

" Hence the *Custom* of the observance of those sequences of sensible qualities, which are similar, can alone convey the *impression*, whence the *idea* of causation results; and thence *necessary connexion* is a

" fancy of the mind," not a relation in nature."

" To prove that *Custom* is the only " *Cause*" of our *belief in causation;* it is perfectly *reasonable* to suppose, that such an *invariable sequence might be interrupted,* for there is no contradiction in imagining an " ARBITRARY" *change in the course of nature.* Yet should a contrary *imagination* resist *reason,* and not conceive *in fact* this interruption as possible to take place; she may again *reconsider* the possibility of nature altering her course, forming no contradiction to *reason.*"

I appeal to those who are acquainted with Mr. Hume's Essays, if this statement be not the sum of the argument—and I also appeal to every man capable of logical accuracy, if it doth not involve every species of illogical sophistry; for,

1st.—There is drawn a general negative conclusion; from an examination of particular instances only. If the adversary may not draw from particular experience the general affirmative conclusion, that *there is a necessary connexion;* neither can Mr. Hume infer a general negative position, that there is *not a necessary connexion* between Cause and Effect. He also deduces a general affirmative conclusion, viz. "*that the future shall invariably resemble the past;* from *particular* instances only *.

2dly.—The mind is directed to infer a conclusion against the general relation of Cause and Effect, by the demonstration of a proposition in nowise inconsistent with it; namely, that *like* sensible qualities, NOT being *like* Causes, might be followed by DIFFERENT Effects†.

3dly.—A general negative conclusion is in fact drawn from negative premises, merely;—(however the illogical method may be disguised both as to manner and diction), for it is concluded there is no proof for the existence of the general rela-

---

* See p. 66, of this Essay.
† See p. 76, ibid.

tion of Cause and Effect between objects;—because experience shows that like sensible qualities are *not* like Causes; and are therefore *not* necessarily connected with like Effects*!

4thly.—The question is *shifted* from the examination of the general relation of Cause and Effect, to that of the criterion for ascertaining the presence of like Causes†.

5thly.—The very proposition is admitted, which is in dispute; in order to serve the purpose of his argument;—first, in the statement that *impressions are the productive Causes of ideas;*—secondly, in supposing the secret powers of an object

---

* It may be seen, that on account of these *particular* and *negative* propositions, (which after all include *that proposition which is in question*) he *really* deduces *there is no such existence, in this relation* AMIDST THINGS— for in the place of the *reality of its existence in nature*, (supposed by their statement to be disproved to reason, and therefore disproved altogether) a "*fancy of it in the mind* alone" is obliged to be substituted in its stead. This " FANCY" is *no connexion* between objects.

† See further, p. 60, and 62, of this Essay.

to be alone *the real productive Causes of its future properties;*—thirdly, in conceiving Nature may alter her course for the express purpose of changing the secret powers; *and that they are changed by such alteration;* —and lastly, in alleging *custom to be the sole Cause* (i. e. producing generating principle) *of the* IDEA *of causation*.†*

6thly.—The proposition that the course of nature may be supposed to change," is used *ambiguously*, signifying indifferently either an uncaused alteration of the SUBSEQUENT *sensible qualities* or of the ANTECEDENT *secret powers* ‡.

7thly, and lastly.—The two chief propositions of the argument are in opposition to each other; for Mr. Hume attempts to establish, *that* CUSTOM *not reason is the prin-*

---

* In these several instances it cannot be contended that Mr. Hume's idea of Cause, is only that of an antecedent; IMPRESSION is supposed not merely *to go before*, but to *create* IDEA; i. e. to be an object absolutely necessary and completely efficient to its production, &c.

† See pages 76, 90, and 146, &c. of this Essay.

‡ See p. 73, ibid.

cipal of causation, whilst he allows REASON to be the sole ground and necessary Cause of this belief.

In presenting the foregoing observations to the reader's attention, I have endeavoured, I hope, without presumption, to show that Mr. Hume's reputation for logical correctness has been overrated. The effect of his work is to astonish by its boldness and novelty;—to allure us by its grace and lightness; his propositions are arranged so artfully, that their illogical connexion is not perceived, and the understanding, without being satisfied, is gradually drawn into inferences from which it would *gladly* but cannot *readily* escape.

If any reader should agree with me in conceiving this scheme to be fallacious, when minutely analyzed, and is thereby enabled to overcome its influence on his mind, I shall consider myself more than repaid for the labour of thought spent in an endeavour towards so desirable an end.

CHAPTER THE FOURTH.

OBSERVATIONS ON DR. BROWN'S ESSAY ON THE DOCTRINE OF MR. HUME.

Dr. Brown's theory merits a particular investigation, and I shall follow him very shortly through each observation he makes on Mr. Hume's doctrine, which he states in *five* propositions. He first of all begins however with his own definition of the relation of Cause and Effect; which does not differ materially from that of Mr. Hume; and has the same inconvenience attending it; viz. *that it will apply to other regular sequences*, than *those which belong to this relation*. " A cause," says he, " is " an object, which immediately precedes " any change, and which existing again in " similar circumstances, will always be im- " mediately followed by a similar change."

And again, " invariableness of antece- " dence, is the element which constitutes " the idea of a cause."

But I ask, how do you get acquainted with this fact? Mr. Hume says he knows it; " because of the habit arising " from past custom, carrying the thought " to an expectation of the future, with a " liveliness of conception equal to the ex- " perience of the past," i. e. there is *uncertain certainty*; for, a lively idea hath not, in a *waking* any more than in a *sleeping* hour, CERTAIN EXISTENCE for its resemblance, without some *other notion* than merely its vivacity to support an *argument for its reality**.

Dr. Brown says, " I know it *from instinctive belief*, arising from the observation of seeing in *any one instance*, certain Effects follow given Causes."

Now I confess, I do not know what " *instinctive belief*" means, except as applied to the mysterious manner in which animals know of the qualities of bodies previous to experience, by some laws be-

---

* This notion is intended to be fully discussed in a future Essay on the nature of external objects.

yond our scrutiny; or at most our conscious belief, of the existence of a simple sensation.

Intuitive belief, I understand; and by it is meant,—that in the relation of the two members of a proposition, the truth is contained in the definition of the terms; and cannot be altered without altering the signs of the ideas, which have been just allowed to stand for them.—But to say that *instinctive*, or *intuitive* belief, can arise in the mind, as a *conclusive proposition*, when it requires *experience*, in order to form some DATA for its *premises;* is to say you believe a thing, without a *reason* for it, and that you are sure of it, because you are sure of it, *although you do want an experiment*, in order to form *a basis for the proposition*, which is to be a *reason* for your *instinctive* conclusion. This is Dr. Brown's Theory.

He is excellent in detecting some of Mr. Hume's fallacies; but in not allowing that the proposition, " like Causes must have like Effects," to be founded on *reason*, is equally guilty of a most important one himself.

The first proposition of Mr. Hume which he examines is, that the relation of Cause and Effect cannot be discovered *à priori*.

To this Dr. Brown assents; and I grant, that the particular qualities which will arise, under new circumstances that bodies shall be placed in, cannot. But the exact nature of the question is here rendered very ambiguous: for the *general* relation of Cause and Effect, is the subject *in question*; but the *question answered*, is whether the *particular* Effects arising from *particular* Causes, can be known; and in *whichever way* it is answered, *it does not form an answer* to the GENERAL one;—for, like Causes in general, might *necessarily be connected* with *like Effects* (of whatever kind they might be); and this proposition known, from some *process of reasoning;* although neither *before* nor *after* experience, the *particular* kind of Effects from given Causes should be discovered. This ambiguity renders the argument nugatory, and it would be tedious and unnecessary to say any thing more upon it.

The second proposition of Mr. Hume's Theory is, that even " after experience the relation of Cause and Effect cannot be discovered by reason." To this Dr. Brown also agrees. The same ambiguity, concerning the nature of the question again prevails; for *reason might be* able to teach us after experience, that the *same* qualities must arise out of the *same objects, when there was nothing to make a difference,* although she should not inform us of the " secrets of nature," and explain to us any better, the mode of the connexion in each particular instance; for if the contrary were true;—if we could know those "secrets" in every particular instance, it could not form a ground, for concluding that " *all* like Causes must have like Effects."—*General conclusions* cannot flow from *particular* premises, whether they be formed by *reason*, or *custom*, or *instinct*.

But Dr. Brown's argument, *against reason*, must be examined more minutely; these are his words; " he who asserts that " A WILL always be *followed* by B, asserts " more than that A always HAS BEEN *followed* by B; and it is *this addition* which " forms the *very essence* of THE RELATION " OF CAUSE AND EFFECT; neither of the " propositions *includes* the other; and as " they have no agreement, *reason*, which " is the sense of agreement, *cannot be applied to them.*"

To represent the relation of Cause and Effect, as A *followed* by B, is a *false view* of the matter. Cause and Effect, might be represented rather by $A \times B = C$, therefore C *is* INCLUDED *in the* MIXTURE OF THE OBJECTS called CAUSE. If C arises once from the *junction of any two bodies;* C must upon every other *like conjunction*, be the *result;* because there is *no alteration in the proportions of the quantities to make a difference;* —C is really *included* in the MIXTURE *of* A *and* B, although, to our senses, we are forced to *note down* (as it were) the SUM arising from their union, *after the observance of their coalescence.* In like manner the results of all arithmetical combinations are *included* in their statements; yet we are obliged to take notice of them separately and subsequently, owing to the imperfection of our senses, in not observing them with sufficient quickness, and *time* being requisite to bring them out to full view and *apparent* in some DISTINCT *shape.* Indeed my whole notion, of the relation of Cause and Effect, is aptly imagined, by the nature of the necessary results, included in the juxta-position of quantities.

But as long as Cause shall be considered ONLY *as an antecedent;* the FUTURE can never be proved to be *included in the* PAST, which yet is truly the case.— For when it comes to be observed, that *Cause means, and really is the creation of* NEW QUALITIES, (from new conjunctions in matter or mind,) then it is perceived that the future is " involved in the past;" for when existing objects *are the same,* they must put on SIMILAR QUALITIES; otherwise *contrary qualities or differences,* would arise of themselves; and " begin their own existences," which is *impossible*, and *conveys a contradiction in terms**. All that *experience* has to do, is to show us, by what passes within ourselves, that there is a *contradiction* in the supposition of *qualities beginning their own existence;* and A CONTRADICTION is never admitted in the *relation of any ideas* that present themselves. The very act of reasoning consists, in such a comparison of our ideas, as will not permit of *inconsistent propositions*†; which would be the case, if " like Causes could produce *other* than like Effects."

So then REASON does establish this beautiful and certain proposition, which

---

* No mathematical reasoning can ever be driven further back, than by showing that the *contrary* of an asserted proposition *is a contradiction in terms.*

† The beginning of every quality is perceived to be only a *change*, upon some objects already in existence; and therefore cannot convey the same notion to the mind, as the *beginning of a quality*, supposed to be *independent of other objects* and NOT to be a change. THE BEGINNING OF EXISTENCE, therefore, cannot appear otherwise than *contrary* to the idea of its *independency* of those objects of which it is a *change*.

is the foundation of all our knowledge;—*That like Causes must ever produce like Effects.*

The third proposition is;—that the relation of Cause and Effect is an object of *belief* alone. To this Dr. Brown also agrees, saying, " any quality which is incapable of being *perceived,* or *inferred,* can result only from an *instinctive principle of faith.*" But I ask how do you know the *future* is invariable? You say from an instinctive principle of faith in observing the *present.* I reply, that it is as impossible to draw an INSTINCTIVE *general conclusion,* from *particular premises,* AS A REASONABLE one. That A follows B, can no more form an *instinct* than a *reason,* for universal certainty of a similar sequence.

The fourth proposition, that the relation of Cause and Effect is believed to exist between objects only after their " *customary*" conjunction is known to us; Dr. Brown combats with such ingenuity, reasons against with such severity of logic, and vanquishes with such skill and power, that all I should attempt to say upon it, would be useless. I can only express my regret, that he could suppose, a notion of *belief*, founded upon the influence of the imagination, rather than of *reason*, to be a *rock*, on which we might build our house, without "*danger of the storm and tempest.*"

Nor is Dr. Brown's "*blind impulse of faith*" a much more secure one. He imagines such a principle to be the foundation of all demonstrative reasoning;—but it is really not so. *Intuitive* propositions are those *included in the very terms*, given to our impressions; and are as true as *they* are, whose truth arises from *simple conscious feelings*, ARBITRARILY named. But INSTINCTIVE propositions, *not so grounded*, and which require some DATA, some *experience*, some *premises*, in which it is confessed they are *not included*, are an absolute contradiction to philosophy and common sense.

The fifth proposition is, "that when "two objects have been frequently observ- "ed in succession, the mind passes readily "from the idea of one to the idea of the "other; the transition in the mind itself "being the impression from which the "idea of the necessary connexion of the "objects as Cause and Effect is de- "rived."

This opinion, namely, "*that an easy transition of thought,*" is the only foundation of the idea of power, Dr. Brown also combats, and conquers; showing in a masterly manner the *illogical* CIRCLE in which Mr. Hume argues.—Indeed it is matter of surprise to reflect on Mr. Hume's reputation, *for logical* precision, when the whole superstructure of his work is built upon the denial of a proposition, which is *assumed as true in the premises;* for in the original inquiry, concerning the method by which we gain *ideas;* Mr. Hume says, it must be from IMPRESSIONS *as their Cause;* i. e. as a "productive principle;" for "their con- "stant conjunction is too frequent to arise

" from chance *;" then examining the nature of the idea of cause, or power; he asks, "from what impression (as its cause) this idea arises" (as its effect)? Thus proving ideas to be " derived" from *impressions*, on account of the *necessary connexion* there exists between them; and then, *disproving* this doctrine of *necessary connexion*, from the *very* notions previously built upon it. It is considered, however, by Dr. Brown, that Mr. Hume's idea of power, although *false*, and only resolvable into a *strong imagination* founded on custom; " a belief not different from that we have in fiction, save

---

* " Let us consider how they stand with regard to " existence, and of the impressions and ideas, which are " Causes and which Effects." TREATISE.—" Such a con-" stant conjunction can never arise from chance, but " proves a dependence of the impressions on the ideas, or " of the ideas on the impressions." TREATISE.—These notions, although not expressed in the *very same words*, are *plainly* found in the Essays. " Every idea is " *copied*," or is " *derived*" from an impression, is precisely the same thought, and which as completely begs the question in dispute, as the passages do which I have quoted from the Treatise; evidently arguing that IMPRESSION is the " productive principle" of *idea*.

in the vivacity of the conception of its objects;" is nevertheless sufficient to guard the doctrine from any charge of excluding the necessity of *Deity for the creation of the universe.*

He seems to think, that as Mr. Hume got hold of the idea of POWER, by *some means or other*, it is immaterial by what means; as any idea of power whatever, would show that a Deity was alike necessary.

But this is false reasoning; if, according to Mr. Hume, we really did, from observing one object always follow another, fall into so strong a fancy, that one was *necessary to produce the other*, as to be unable to avoid the conclusion of their invariable and absolute dependence on each other; yet upon the supposition of once knowing this conclusion to be only the effect of a habit of mind, arising from an association of ideas; (a fancy, a custom of thought); we should nevertheless consider that the objects in nature might be perfectly independent of each other; and therefore could not draw any conclusion in favour of the necessity of a Creator, as the "productive principle" of the universe.

For should the circumstance of B following A, in all alphabets, generate in our minds the false notion that A *causes* B, yet if afterwards we should discover that these letters were not *truly necessary* to each other, and that in nature *any other letter* than B might *follow* A; although after such discovery, B might always be *suggested* on the *appearance* of A; yet not only would the notion of *causation* be really destroyed, if it arose from the *invariableness of their antecedence and subsequence;* but upon the supposition of the contrary, and that notwithstanding the conviction of the judgment, the *fancy of their mutual necessary dependence held its ground;* still we should not justify such an example as fit to be followed in ALL *our other expectations;* or thence conclude, that *all things we know of*, required necessarily their *antecedents*. No;—this *fancy of power*, without *knowledge of it;* this imagination of productive principle, without an enlightened judgment concerning its absolute necessity, cannot be all that is necessary, to any arguments that are founded on the belief of POWER."

A false and fanciful idea of power, of cause, and of connexion, is just as unsubstantial for their support, as though these words were absolutely " without any meaning."

The denial of the idea of power, as of truly a " productive principle," as of a *former and generator of new qualities in matter*, and the consideration of it as only " *a custom of mind*," does *not prevent the doctrine, as Dr. Brown seems to think it may, from involving the most dangerous consequences.*

How such an idea of power as Mr. Hume's, should give us the " consolation, and the peace, and the happiness, and the virtue of a filial confidence in the great

Father of mankind," is hard to discover? A faith like this, would not go far in affording men that " security which has more to do with our happiness, than any present earthly enjoyment!"

CHAPTER THE FIFTH.

OBSERVATIONS ON MR. LAWRENCE'S LECTURES.

SECTION THE FIRST.

I shall now proceed to offer a few observations on a modern author, (Mr. Lawrence,) who in his Physiological Lectures, eagerly seizes upon Dr. Brown's definition of the relation of Cause and Effect; which he imagines well adapted to an explanation of the properties of life.

In his 3d Lecture, p. 81, Mr. Lawrence says, " we can only trace, in this notion of
" necessary connexion, the fact of certainty
" or universality of concurrence; therefore
" it is we may assert the living muscular
" fibre is irritable, and the living nervous
" fibre is sensible. Nothing more than this
" is meant when a necessary connexion is
" asserted between the properties of sensi-

"bility, and irritability, and the structures
"of living muscular and nervous fibres."

And again, page 79, "The only reason
"we have for asserting in any case that
"any property belongs to any substance,
"is the certainty or universality with which
"we find the substance, and the property
"in question, accompanying each other.—
"Thus we say gold is ductile, yellow, solu-
"ble in nitro-muriatic acid, because we
"have always found gold when pure to be
"so—we assert the living muscular fibres
"to be irritable, and the living nervous
"fibres to be sensible for the same reason.
"The evidence of the two propositions
"presents itself to my mind as unmarked
"by the faintest shade of difference." According to the theory of the foregoing pages
of this Essay, there is the greatest difference
between the evidence of the two propositions just quoted.

An object is here defined; "a combined mass of qualities, determined to
the senses from unknown causes in nature,
to which an arbitrary name is affixed." But

property which is synonymous with Effect, " is the yet *untried*, or unobserved quality, which *will* arise upon the mixture of that mass with other objects."

The *necessary connexion*, therefore, of a *name*, with the *qualities which it designates*, is no more than the connexion of an *arbitrary sound* with an *object*, or in other words with the *unknown causes in nature*, which determine the qualities that affect our senses; and which must be " necessarily connected with it" so long as we do not contradict ourselves in terms; or at least whilst we agree not to alter our terms. But the *necessary connexion* of an *object*, and its further *properties*, (or effects,) viz. those which are produced by its union with another object, arises from the obligation that certain combinations of qualities have to beget upon their *junction* with other combinations, certain NEW QUALITIES; and this *necessary connexion* must take place between the like objects on all future occasions, from the obligation that *like Causes have to produce like Effects*. The connexion of gold with fusibility, ductility, &c. is of the former kind of connexion, viz. that of a *name* for certain enumerated *qualities, en masse**.—The connexion of sentiency with the *live* nerve, is of the latter kind. The former is a *necessary* but *arbitrary* connexion; the latter is considered as a NECESSARY *Effect*, from certain combined and efficient *causes*.

SECTION THE SECOND.

Should it be objected, the word *gold*, does not stand as a mere *arbitrary* sign for *certain enumerated qualities*, but as a term, for *a portion of extended matter*, which will exhibit upon trial, *certain properties peculiar to itself*, I admit, that it is perfectly philosophical to consider the subject in this point of view; for either *a noun* as a *name*, may be considered as a sign, for *all* the qualities and properties understood to be under the term;—or as a sign, merely standing for

---

* See Locke's Essay on Human Understanding, Chap. 3. b. 6. Sec. 35.

the qualities of the genus;—then the noun is still only necessarily connected in the sense of an *arbitrary* connexion, *with the qualities which compose the genus*,—and the *mass of qualities*, which combine to form this *object*, are afterwards necessarily connected as *a Cause;* when in its conjunction, with any other objects; it puts on further qualities, which then are its *effects*, or *properties*. In this sense, *gold*, mixed with light, (some of whose rays it reflects,) is necessarily yellow; mixed with heat, (in different degrees,) it is ductile, and fusible; mixed with N. M. acid, it is soluble.

If this should be the sense, which I do not think it is, of Mr. Lawrence in his passage on gold—it is true there may be " no difference between the evidence for the two propositions;" for both objects are *necessarily* and *invariably* connected with their effects or properties.

But neither of them are to be regarded, as *only* so connected with their properties *in future, because they have been invariably concurrent in past time.*

Mr. Lawrence, no more than Dr. Brown, or Mr. Hume, can predicate of *the* FUTURE, from *the past*, unless under the relation of Cause and Effect, as of a truly *productive principle, with a quality produced.*

I would further observe, that the arbitrary connexion of a name, with a certain number of similar enumerated qualities, requires no proof for its assertion; such qualities shall be gold, and such others lead and copper, if we please to call them so. But the necessary connexion of an object and its further *properties*, when combined with other objects, requires *experiment to prove its truth.*

Also the *definition* of the arbitrary name, is *absolute.*—Because the proposition in which it is contained is identical; such qualities, are gold—and gold is the enumeration of such qualities. But the definition of an object in respect to its exhibition of *further qualities in different combi-*

nations with other objects, is *conditional;* it being understood that it will not hold, unless the *circumstances are similar* upon each occasion, that have any *power to affect them**.

SECTION THE THIRD.

It is plain that Mr. Lawrence has overlooked these distinctions, where there are such manifest differences, on account of his " becoming acquainted with Dr. Brown's Essay on Cause and Effect," which he considers as " so simple and logical that any attempt at direct opposition would " be utterly hopeless;" and has quoted a long passage in a note as a proof of this, and as a support of the doctrine he is laying down in the text.

In this passage are the three following sentences, which I shall not apologize for inserting; since the consequences of a hasty adoption, of what I consider FALSE *instead of* LOGICAL *deduction, and confused*

---

* See Locke's Essay, Chap. 6. Book 4. Sec. 8 and 9; where unexpectedly I find he perfectly coincides with me.

instead of "simple" argument into important practical theories, cannot be too strongly deprecated, and I wish to give my reader full possession of the grounds of my reasoning.

The 1st consists in the definition of the relation of Cause and Effect, which I have already commented on, in the former Chapter against Dr. Brown.

" A cause is that which immediately
" precedes any change, and which existing
" at any time in similar circumstances, has
" been always, and will be always followed
" by a similar change."

" Priority, in the sequence observed and
" *invariableness* of antecedence in the *past*
" and *future* sequences supposed, are the
" *only* elements combined in the notion of
" a cause."

2dly. Of property, " the words property
" and quality admit of exactly the same de-
" finition, expressing only a certain relation
" of invariable antecedence and conse-

"quence in changes that take place on the
" presence of the substance to which they
" are ascribed."

3dly. " The powers, properties or qua-
" lities of a substance are not to be re-
" garded as any thing superadded to the
" substance, or distinct from it. They are
" *only* the substance itself considered in re-
" lation to various changes that take place
" when it exists in peculiar circumstances."

Hence Mr. Lawrence concludes, p. 81,
" That although induced to ascribe the
" constant concomitance of a substance
" and its properties to *some necessary con-*
" *nexion* between them, yet we can only
" trace in this notion, the fact of cer-
" tainty or universality of concurrence.
" *Nothing more* than this can be meant
" when a *necessary connexion* is asserted
" between the properties of sensibility, and
" irritability, and the structures of living
" muscular and nervous fibres."

Now I must shortly bring to my readers recollection, that I have already shown that

Dr. Brown's definition which predicates *invariableness* in relation to *future* sequences, is not supported by his argument, as no *past* experience *merely*, could prove it;—it being *illogical* to draw general conclusions from particular premises.—I have also, I think, shown that our knowledge of the *future*, arises from its being " *involved*" in the past; on account of *Cause being truly a productive principle*, and *Effects or properties* truly *produced* qualities, so that necessary connexion becomes a very different relation from either a *past or future sequence* of events, and signifies the " close bond" between the creator and created.

Had Mr. Lawrence, however, paid more attention than he has done to the *concluding* sentence I have quoted from Dr. Brown, he had not engrafted these errors into his system :—for nothing can be more just and beautiful than to say of the properties of a substance, " that they are only " the *substance itself* in relation to *various* " *changes* which take place, *when it exists* " *in peculiar circumstances.*"—But such an idea is at variance with all his own previous definitions and arguments on the subject, for if " the powers, properties, or qualities " of a substance are not to be regarded as " any thing superadded to the substance, " or distinct from it, but only the substance " itself, considered in relation to various " changes which take place when it exists " in peculiar circumstances," then these properties and qualities cannot be *after* itself; but are *necessarily* connected *with*, because *inhering* in it, and brought out to view when *mixed* with the qualities of *other objects*.

SECTION THE FOURTH.

Now as the muscle and nerve can and do exist as organized beings, without irritability and sentiency when under death, so when as substances, they are placed under that condition called *life*, and are then only capable of putting on these qualities of irritability and sentiency, it must be by a *truly necessary connexion*, between life and these qualities. Irritability and sentiency are verily new powers and beings *created* by efficient, *creating* circumstances. Sen-

sation and all its variety, is not an effect without a cause; and *life* is that object without which it will not exist in the *nerve;* and therefore according to the doctrine laid down in this Essay, is a true cause for it: being *one* of the objects *absolutely necessary* and efficient to *that* result in *certain circumstances;*—although what the WHOLE of those conditions may be, the *combination* of which is needful, may possibly ever remain beyond the scrutiny of man. Should Mr. Lawrence retort, that the phrase " the living nerve," stands *merely* as a *sign* of enumerated *qualities* and properties found together, in the way that I have said *gold* may stand as a *sign* for those that lie under that term; that it is in this sense he compares the two propositions concerning them; and in this sense, he alleges there is no difference in the evidence for the *only kind* of necessary connexion there exists between an *object* and its properties?

I answer the very statement of the proposition " the *living nerve* is *sentient*," *assigns a cause* and *producing principle* for sensation; for by placing an adjective before a noun, it becomes a *qualified noun*. And the qualities beneath the whole term are a mass of *altered* qualities, which alteration, is alleged to be *efficient* to the production of a new mode of existence; viz. that of sensation.

Thus (to use a familiar illustration) the saying a *bilious* man is *choleric*, assigns *vile* as the *cause* of anger, and it would be puerile after such a proposition, to add, that " however strong the feeling may be, that " there is the close bond of Cause and Ef-" fect between these objects, yet it is a " mistake to suppose it." This would but be a subsequent denial of *what the statement previously asserted*.

Whereas *gold*, or any other noun, when it stands as a sign for any collection of qualities, and properties; is neither a cause nor an object; it is a word, a *name* merely, and when thus placed as the subject of a proposition, of which the qualities stand as the predicate, signifies, that by such a name, shall such masses, being found together and set apart from other collections, be signified*.

This distinction between a *qualified*, and *unqualified* noun, on account of the different *nature* of the *connexion* of the predicate of the proposition, with its subject, Mr. Lawrence did not take notice of; or he would not have thought " there was not the faintest shade of difference" between the two propositions he states, in this respect.

SECTION THE FIFTH.

But this is not the most important error in Mr. Lawrence's system, arising from false notions, concerning the relation of Cause and Effect; for by a strange sort of contradiction, in philosophy, although he denies that *any cause* can be found, among those things which are invariably together, for the properties they exhibit; yet he makes no difficulty in inferring that the *whole causes* are supposed to be found

---

* See Locke's Essay in several places, especially Book 3. Chap. 8. Sec. 2. compared with Chap. 9. Sec. 12, 13, and 17. and Chap. 10. Sec. 20, 21, and 22.

from the mere circumstance of their invariable coalesence; insomuch that *no extraneous* cause need be sought for.— The sum of his argument is, "*There is no such thing as* CAUSE *and* EFFECT, *to be perceived between the objects with which we are acquainted. It is idle to say we have found a Cause; it is still more idle to look for it.*—*Objects are found to be amassed qualities and properties, which have invariably existed together in past time, and for that reason will do so in future; but as for a productive principle, it is unworthy of a philosopher to expect it, or to seek for it; or to need it, in order to account for any appearances. We have objects, variously diversified—this is all and this is enough!*"

It is hence, (so Mr. Lawrence argues,) absurd *to seek a Cause* for sensation or thought, although no efficient one is pretended to be assigned, in the union of the powers of life with organization. The living nerve is an object having sensation—"*this is all and this is enough.*"—Whereas there must be causes for every thing, and sometimes a *vast multitude of objects are wanted,* before their *mutual bearings* and *mixtures* with each other operate so as to *produce* any peculiar existence. The highest, and the greatest we know of is, *sensation, and its varieties;* and although we know that life is *wanted* as a *cause* without which it cannot exist in *this world in the nervous system;* yet we have no notion of *all* the objects that may be necessary to its creation.

Of all philosophical errors, the substitution of false, partial, or insufficient causes for the production of an end or object, is the most dangerous, because so liable to escape detection; and the idleness of the mind which prosecutes with reluctance difficult researches into remote proofs; its impatience which eagerly grasps at the readiest solution of a doubt; and its pride, so prone to triumph indiscreetly at the glimpse of a discovery supposed to be complete; for ever occasion it to be guilty of that mode of sophistry scholastically termed *non causa—pro causa.*

And this is *truly* the amount of Mr. Lawrence's error—for with all his denial that there are such things as *cause* and *necessary connexion*, he virtually assigns a "*false cause*" for sensation, because he asserts that *all* is found that is *necessary* in order to it*.

Now the truth is, that nature affords not experiment, or data enough to show, what are the *whole* causes necessary; i. e. *all* the objects required, whose *junction* is necessary to *sentiency as the result.*—For as the words *life*, and *nerve*, stand only for a few sensible qualities, whereby they affect us; so does it appear there is no existing definition of them, no possible experiment which can be made on their nature, sufficient to afford premises wide enough to admit the conclusion, that sentiency shall result from their conjunction only, and shall not be able to exist without them.

* Mr. Lawrence says, there is no more reason to search for a cause for sensation or life—than for attraction or electricity—yet these powers must have Causes, and philosophers have searched for them; and if they have given over the inquiry, it is because they despair of success.

SECTION THE SEVENTH.

If indeed the powers of matter in general, (whatever matter may be,) were sufficient to elicit sentiency when placed under *arrangement* and mixed with life, then the true causes for it are assigned, and found. But we cannot *prove* this. If on the contrary, the essential qualities of matter arranged and in motion be not thought sufficient to account for so extraordinary a difference as that between conscious and unconscious being, then there must be a *particular* cause for it: which cause must be considered an immaterial cause, that is, a *principle, power, being*, an unknown quality *denied* to exist in matter.—This must have a name, and may be called *soul*, or *spirit*. And this statement, really contains the whole argument either way. It is on this point, that not only *here*, but in an after Lecture (" on the functions of the brain,") Mr. Lawrence betrays a want of philosophical precision, by denying that any cause beyond the brain is necessary to thought, on account of the impossibility of assigning the *time* of its union with the body; whereas a Cause must have originally been necessary, upon the creation of man, for the phenomenon in question; and the capacity of sensation may, as a component part of the whole animal mass, be always generated with it, yet retain its individuality, after having once been formed with each being;—analogous to the whole plan of nature, in other respects;—analogous to the physical individuality of all the millions of mankind, each of which was formed of the general clay;—analogous to the separate, and particular properties, which wait upon the differences of vegetable life, where every various plant is expanded from similar juices.

But I must be true to my own doctrine in all its bearings; and as I have said, that in order to form the *proximate cause* of any event, a *junction or mutual mixture of all* the objects *necessary to it must take place;* so I conceive it to be impossible, but that a *distinct* and *different* action of the brain (without which organ there is no sensation in man, and all thought is but a mode of it) must be *synchronous* with whatever other powers are also necessary for that result; viz. sensation and thought with their varieties. I say, the junction must be *synchronous*—for sensation is an *effect*, and must require the union of those objects whose mixed qualities elicit it.

Now those causes *not* contained in matter, may be called mind, or soul. I have said also, that a different action of brain is wanted for *each variety of thought and sensation;* and so it must, because there must be a *separate* or different cause, for every *separate or diverse* Effect in nature, as before discussed. And thus the brain becomes the *exponent of the soul;* or is *in the same proportion in its actions,* as the actions of mind: and thus what is termed *association of ideas,* must have *corresponding unions,* in the actions of the brain.

Now Mr. Lawrence contradicts at once his own arguments for materialism, as well as nature, and fact; when he says (tauntingly) " thus we come to diseases of " an immaterial being! for which suitably

" enough *moral* treatment has been recom-
" mended," inferring thereby the *absurdity
of moral treatment*, to a *material mind*.

Now moral treatment, according to his *own notion* of *only a material* capacity for thought, might still be proper, as it would still act on that *material capacity for thought*,—and though " arguments, syllogisms, and sermons," might not reach it, of an *ordinary kind;* yet, the persuasions of friendship; the influence of beauty, and of love; the pleasures of social intercourse; the calm discussions of reason; scenes that please the imagination, or enchant the sense, will reach it, and do. Nevertheless all this is " *moral treatment*," and which yet requires the brain and nervous system. In short, to address the mind is to address the body, which *instantly* acts along and with it, not *after* it. And to address the body is to address the mind—for *every sensation*, however popularly called *bodily;* requires *mind*, equally with thought as a cause for it, and is not merely to be considered as a simple being, or feeling, beginning and ending in itself; but as intimately *associating with those of a* LIKE KIND, *which certain* THOUGHTS *are capable of exciting, and as having, therefore, a most material agency, when first in order, by suggesting such specific thoughts.*—This mode of thinking on the subject I know not that any have sufficiently heeded, much less cultivated.

It is to be lamented that the use of pure metaphysics has not been more strictly adopted into the researches of physiology, since the just application of these sciences to each other, would tend to the advancement of both.—Nor have the talents and genius of Mr. Lawrence exempted him, in this respect, from the common failure.

For (in his Lecture on the functions of the brain,) he is guilty of a very great oversight in supposing philosophers speak of an *immaterial* being as wanted for *thought*, and *not for sensation*.—Instead of which Mr. Locke, Bishop Butler, David Hartley, Bishop Berkeley, all distinctly argue that matter in motion, not seeming *cause* sufficient for the most *simple sensation*, therefore *spirit* is wanted to that end; which is merely a name for the cause desired: and this mistake shows the little attention he has paid to these authors. But I consider it as impossible that any material improvement should be made in the method of applying philosophy to physiology, as long as men argue, that in every action of the senses, the *body* acts BEFORE *the mind and* UPON *it*. And *vice versa*, as I have heard it contended in argument " *that the actions of the memory, the imagination, and the reasoning powers, begin in the mind, exist entirely in the mind, act before the body, and upon it.*" Nor will it advance, as long as any anxiety among materialists makes them *wish* to show *all* is body. Or, on the contrary, if whilst religious men are fearful that their dearest hopes may fail them, in case *any* thing of *body* is wanted, in order to *thought*. Whereas religion is not concerned in this matter so much as they imagine. If immortality is man's inheritance, it is not as a natural birthright. The meanest worm must *feel and think* as well as man, and yet may not be immortal—If it is his; it is a *gift*, which the Giver has power enough to make good by ways unseen to us; but not surely by conveying to man a power *so indiscerptible, indivisible, &c.* that he becomes a rival to his own omnipotence and " *shall not surely die.*"

SECTION THE EIGHTH.

But to return from this digression which yet was necessary, in order to represent, the whole of Mr. Lawrence's mistaken reasoning on this branch of the subject, I shall only at present further observe, that as the *nature of life* is become a question of great interest, I must reserve a few more observations upon it for another chapter, as Mr. Lawrence has given *various*, and apparently, *inconsistent* definitions of that word. Nor must it be supposed irrelevant to the present subject so to do, for I think his erroneous views in this respect arise also on account of his not supposing that a real efficient cause is necessary to be assigned for *life* any more than for *sensation*. Therefore all philosophers are reckoned absurd, who have hitherto endeavoured, or who still continue, to seek for the proximate cause of it; it being considered by him quite sufficient to look upon it as a *circumstance only concurring with organization,*—whereas " there must be a cause for every thing," *and a cause for that cause*, backwards towards an uncreated Essence.

But every step gained in the knowledge of causes, (i. e. of what objects are necessary in order to the *production* of another) is of exquisite value, and it is pity if a false philosophy should succeed in slackening the emulation of inquiring minds upon this subject, which is one of the highest moment to human health and happiness.

I shall therefore, in order to show that I do not mistake my author, take an opportunity of placing together these definitions, &c. in his own words: but in order to be brief, leave out entirely all foreign matter with which they are interspersed, and which prevent the exact noticing of the contradictions that appear to be among them.

CHAPTER THE SIXTH.

SECTION THE FIRST.

I RESUME the subject by saying, that it is difficult to controvert Mr. Lawrence's opinion of the nature of life, because his definitions bear no resemblance to each other. They are as follows:

(Lecture 1st, p. 7.) " That life then, or " the assemblage of all the functions, is " immediately *dependant on organization,* " appears to me as clear, as that the pre " sence of the sun causes the light of day; " and to suppose that we could have light " without that luminary, would not be " more unreasonable than to conceive that " life is independent of the animal body, in " which the vital phenomena are observed.'

Lecture 2d, p. 61. " To talk of life as " independent of an animal body, to speak " of a function without reference to an ap- " propriate organ, is physiologically absurd " —it is looking for an effect without a " cause."

(Lecture 3d, p. 81.) "The living muscular fibre is irritable. The living nervous fibre is sensible."—(p. 82.) "To call life a *property of organization* would be unmeaning, it would be nonsense. The primary or elementary animal structures are endowed with vital properties; their combinations compose the animal organs, in which by means of the vital properties of the component elementary structures, the animal functions are carried on."

Lecture 4th, p. 92. "The body is composed of solids and fluids;—*the component elements of which nitrogen is a principal one,* united in numbers of 3, 4, or more, easily pass into new combinations; and *are, for the most part, readily convertible into fluid or gas.*"

(P. 93.) "Life presupposes organization."

(Ibid.) Again; "Living bodies exhibit a constant internal motion; whilst this motion lasts, the body is said to be alive

"—when it ceases, the organic structures
"then yield to the chemical affinities of
"the surrounding elements.".

SECTION THE SECOND.

Now, surely, it is a contradiction to say, life is " *dependant on organization,*" as light is upon the sun, and yet that it is " *unmeaning*" and *nonsense*, to call life a *property of it* *. It is a second contradiction to say, that life is *dependant as a function*, upon an animated body†; when the body could not be animated without it; or that as " *assembled functions,*" it is " dependant
" on organization, as light is dependant on
" the sun ‡." When life is so far from consisting in " the *assembled functions,*" that none of the functions can take place without life,—and thus it is wanted as a quality, or *being, first in order to coalesce* and form a junction with the organs in order to their action. Accordingly, although life may never be found without organization, because life requires *its co-operation in order to a certain result*, yet life is not thence *dependant*

* Lect. 3. p. 82.   † Lect. 2. p. 61.
‡ Lect. 1. p. 7.

on it, as an *effect* upon *its cause*, as light is upon the sun, which is never above the horizon without its brilliant attendant.—But many a beautiful and youthful set of organs are *perfect*, without animation.—This error arises entirely from considering that as Cause and Effect are *things that go together;* so *things that go together* are to be considered as in that relation. Whereas vast varieties of objects, have been invariably together in past time, which are not Cause and Effect; and as *past invariableness will not answer for the future*, may not in future be so found. *Joint Causes are always found together; joined qualities also from a common Cause:* and many objects have hitherto always been found together, from an arbitrary position of them, independent of the relation of Cause and Effect, as the letters of the alphabet, &c.

It is a third contradiction to say, that the elementary structures are endowed with vital properties*, and yet to reduce them into the inorganic matters of nitrogen and gas†.

* Lect. 3. p. 82. † Lect. 4. p. 92.

In my opinion, the only clear and valuable definition is the latter one; viz. "life is a constant internal motion, which enables a body to assimilate new and separate old particles, and prevents it from yielding to the chemical affinities of the surrounding elements." Such a definition as this, comprehends *all the ideas* under the *term*, without begging the question of its cause, or mentioning what it is found with.

It has also the merit of universal *comprehension*, as it comprehends vegetable as well as animal life—and of *exclusion*, not suiting any thing else but itself. It thence leaves free the varieties of the functions, to arise from appropriate organs; and it proves that either *all living* beings must be *sentient*, or else a *further cause* must be sought for *sensation* than *mere life*.

SECTION THE THIRD.

That "life must presuppose organization*," is another proposition of Mr. Lawrence's, which I must also deny;

---

* Lect. 4. p. 93.

and that because life is absolutely necessary both for its formation and support. Without life in the parents, the organs could not have been formed; and without life they cannot act in their juxta-position, upon the surrounding *elements*, either before or after birth, in order to their growth and support. Yet when life is once *given*, the *use of the organs is absolutely necessary to keep it up.*

Thus combustible matters may be heaped upon each other, yet neither warmth nor light succeed; but let an "*extra cause*" kindle the pile, then the flame may be kept alive for ever, by the constant *addition* of such substances.—In like manner life as we find it, as a perpetual flame, must be kept up and transmitted, whilst the proper objects for its support are administered: but for its original *Cause*, we must go back, until some extraneous power is referred to as its first parent. It is an *Effect;* it begins to be in all we know and have known, yet it is wanted in its own turn as a cause, and as a quality already in being, to mix and unite with the gross elements of brute matter, for the formation and continuance of all animated nature.

We are told that "*God breathed into man the breath of life,*" and here philosophy supports Scripture, for the organs must originally have been kindled into life by a power, equal to giving them that internal vigour and motion, capable of enabling them to act afterwards for themselves, upon the objects which surrounded them. Then the living lungs could play upon the air, the living stomach be hungry and assimilate its food, the living heart beat, and the living blood circulate through every vein, and become capable of transmitting *the principle* communicated to it, to similar natures, without any assignable termination.

My notion of life therefore agrees in this respect with that of Mr. Lawrence, viz. " That it is a peculiar inward motion of the " organs."—And I consider it further, as continually propagated through the species, and mixing with the newly evolved forms of arranged matter; *and that it is kept up, as long as the organs remain sound, and they are placed in fit circumstances for their respective actions.*

But men and animals are all of them *Effects*, and the first of each kind *and its life could not have begun of itself*,—nor yet as *Effects*, could they go back to all eternity, for *they might as well be here in time without causes*, as in eternity; Effects, however far removed from the present date, are still Effects; are still only *new qualities* from the *junction of previous objects;* which objects (the Causes) could not have been the same with the qualities, (the Effects).

The first cause of life therefore must be " extraneous" to any of the bodies among which it is found. For at their first creation, and in order to act their *parts* as it were, the organs must not only have been *arranged* but have *lived*, and this life communicated to them at the same time, and probably by the same forming powers, as a joint quality with their arrangement. Thus a clock may be ever so well put together, but the different instruments will not perform their *functions*, without an "*extraneous power*" originally to put the pendulum in motion:—then afterwards the pendulum by the *natural physical laws between it and the surrounding objects*, will *continue* to beat; whilst also the motion *of the other* mechanical instruments forms a *part* of the *whole* power necessary to keep it going, though not wanted *at first* to that end. This would form such a *circle* of Cause and Effect, as would be inexplicable, except upon the principle of the original *former* and *mover* being "*extraneous*" to both.

In like manner, all qualities of existing objects, which now play on each other as mutual Cause and Effect, the lungs, which are necessary to the heart, and the heart to to the lungs,—and both to the action of the brain, and the action of the brain to both;—life which is necessary to sensation, and the movement of the whole;—and sensation, and the movement of the whole to life, must all of them (in order to explain such phenomena) have originally had their builder, and mover, not contained in their own powers.

Now the proximate cause for the principle, or motion termed life, *may*, and ought to be inquired into by physiologists.

But that it is only, and *essentially*, the result, and consequence, or property or element, of the being to whose results, qualities and finest elements, it is necessary in order to give them birth; is a contradiction, inadmissible in the application of abstract demonstration to the objects of life.

SECTION THE FOURTH.

But as long as the notions of Mr. Hume shall prevail, inquiries of this nature will be instituted in vain; nor indeed is there any received doctrine upon the relation of Cause and Effect, which can be securely used, as an efficient instrument in the advancement of science.

Bishop Berkeley thought a Cause must necessarily be *active*, and so a *spirit!* And it is universally imagined that a Cause is, in its very essence, *before* its Effects.

There is also, a notion that one object is *sufficient* to an event; when many are perhaps wanted in order to produce it.

I pretend not to have found the whole nature of this relation;—But I shortly recapitulate what I have advanced.

1st.—The junction of two or more qualities or objects is wanted to every new creation of a new quality.

2dly.—That any *one* of the qualities or objects needful in order to the formation of another, may be termed a *Cause*, because *absolutely necessary*, and, when all the other needful circumstances are duly placed with which it is to unite, *efficient* to its production.

But, 3dly. The *whole* number of objects existing, which are necessary to it, may also, under one complex idea, be deemed *the one whole* cause necessary.

4thly.—The *union of these*, is the proximate Cause of, and is *one* with the Effect.

5thly.—The *objects* therefore are *before* the Effects, but the *union of them* is *in* and *with* the Effects.

This ambiguity, arising from the necessity of naming each object, wanted to an end, and all that are wanted to it, and the junction necessary to it, the *Cause* of it, is a fruitful source of error in every branch of analytical philosophy.

6thly.—When Effects or *new qualities* are once formed, they may re-act as Causes, in order to keep up the original objects, which contributed to their formation.

7thly.—Although the very word Effect implies a *change* in qualities, yet among a set of new qualities formed, *all* of them are not therefore entirely changed.

The spark first elicited from the tinder, is kept separate, as to its appearance, its warmth and light, amidst all the alteration, in which it involves the objects it approaches.

8thly.—*It is not necessary, however,* that *any* of the Effects, *should resemble any of the objects*, by whose union they are caused;—and in general, an entire mixture, junction and concussion of qualities, involves the whole original objects in ruins, whilst it strikes out a vast many new and altered ones, creating other masses, other complex objects, totally unlike those whose union was their Cause. On the other hand, it sometimes appears that nature intends to render one individual essence, the prime object intended to be preserved; and therefore in its mixture with others, ordains that they shall only administer to it, by contributing to the perpetual nourishment, support, and increase of its qualities; as in the growth of plants and animals; or the vigour, improvement, character, individuality, &c. of the sentient principle.——

SECTION THE FIFTH.

But to conclude;—Mr. Lawrence's error lies, 1st, in the adoption and application of the principle, that invariability of concurrence, is of the samenature as the relation of Cause and Effect, object and property; which is the result of an argument in a circle, and which cannot be too severely deprecated, however authorized, by the illogical definitions of Mr. Hume and Dr. Brown.

And, 2dly. In concluding that because *one or more Causes* known to be necessary to an end, are discovered, therefore *all* are discovered, which is to draw general conclusions from particular premises. Did an ignorant person, unacquainted with the method of forming a mirror, consider it as no more than polished glass;—did he only observe that it reflected images when polished, and that injuring the polish prevented their reflection, he might form a proposition very similar to that of Mr. Lawrence, and say; *polished glass reflects the images when presented to it;* polish, and glass, and reflection, always go together; and as this is the case, we need not seek for any "*extrinsic aid*," to the production of reflected images from its surface. But we know that *extrinsic aid is wanted to the whole Effect.* And indeed before a reflected image from a mirror can be attained, let the mind pause, and wonder at the great variety of objects necessary to cause it. Can we much better enumerate those that may be requisite, to the formation of the most simple modes of sensation? Do we know the qualities of matter, when we use the term? Do we know the reason of all its varieties when we name them by some feeble impressions they make on our organs? As unperceived by the senses, have we the least idea of what is in matter in general, or in the *nerve* in particular, or in the formation of animals, or in the nature of life, that we should suppose nothing more is made use of for so extraordinary a difference, as that between sentient and insentient beings, than *arrangement*, (i. e. organization,) and *motion*, (or whatever other mode of being is termed life?) Certain it is, there is no experiment can be made on animated nature, which shall prove what are *all*, and *only* those objects, which may be necessary to SENSATION; or whether the sensient principle *be like*, or altogether unlike the *Effect*, SENSATION; and indeed in any experiment which destroyed the life and the nerve, if this principle should continue to exist, our senses could not descry it.

SECTION THE SIXTH.

What probable arguments may be advanced upon the matter, is foreign to the object of this Essay, and I shall not now enter upon them; but conclude by expressing my astonishment, that Mr. Hume's and Dr. Brown's definition of the relation of Cause and Effect, should have continued so long, admired, adopted, and unanswered.

The necessary connexion of Cause and Effect, and our knowledge of it, in opposition to mere *fancy or custom*, is the governing proposition in every science. In vain should we look for improvement in any, *could we run the risk of so vital* a mistake, as to suppose that objects, however frequently conjoined, were *therefore necessarily connected*, or, on the contrary, that in the necessary production of qualities, there was no more than an experienced conjunction of them, and that they might change their places by a " change in the course of nature."

I have endeavoured to show, that any one junction of bodies in fit circumstances for what is termed the experimentum crucis, may be sufficient to establish where the power lies towards the production of certain qualities,—that ordinary life affords such experiment to the mind; and that without it, constant conjunctions of antecedent and subsequent objects, will not prove where the Cause of an Effect is. Conjunctions, however frequent, may be separable both in fact and fancy; Cause and Effect, a changed object with its changed qualities, are inseparable in both.

Let then the following just propositions be again received—

That objects cannot begin their own existences.

That like objects, must ever have like qualities.

That like Causes, must generate like Effects.

And that objects, of which we have had no experience, must resemble those of which we have had experience, for that the course of Nature continues uniformly the same.

These are the only true foundations of scientific research, of practical knowledge, and of belief in a creating and presiding Deity.

THE END.

ERRATA.

Page 12 *line* 16 *for* " a," *read* " or."
    37 — 32 *dele* " by."
    51 — 25 — " of."
    52 — 1 — " ,"
    57 — 7 *for* " exists," *read* " exist."
    74 — 13 *dele* " with."
    77 — 22 — " else."
    90 — 22 *for* " shew," *read* " shewing."
   104 — 2 — " excited," *read* " elicited."